Strategic Alliances of the Seven False Crowns

Unmask the Enemy's Coordinated Deceptions and Step Into Kingdom Authority

By

Dr. Ron M. Horner

Strategic Alliances of the Seven False Crowns

Unmask the Enemy's Coordinated Deceptions
and Step Into Kingdom Authority

By

Dr. Ron M. Horner

LifeSpring International Ministries
PO Box 5847
Pinehurst, North Carolina 28374
www.RonHorner.com

Strategic Alliances of the Seven False Crowns

Unmask the Enemy's Coordinated Deceptions and Step Into Kingdom Authority

Requests for bulk sales discounts, editorial permissions, or other information should be addressed to:

LifeSpring Publishing
PO Box 5847
Pinehurst, NC 28374 USA

Additional copies available at RonHorner.com

ISBN 13 TP: 978-1-953684-78-3
ISBN 13 eBook: 978-1-953684-79-0

Cover Design by Darian Horner Design
(www.darianhorner.com)
Image: 123rf.com #239820784

First Edition: March 2026

10 9 8 7 6 5 4 3 2 1 0

Printed in the United States of America

Table of Contents

Acknowledgments

Thanks to Stephanie, the Chief Operating Officer of LifeSpring International Ministries for her willingness to engage Heaven with me to unveil truths and breakthrough revelation on behalf of the Body of Christ.

Thanks also to my wife, Adina. You're the best.

———— ∞ ————

Preface

In early 2025, I found myself teaching about crowns. With my assistant, Stephanie we started with a study of the various crowns in the Bible —why were they given, to whom, what did they represent, and so on. I learned that crowns are not just for when we get to Heaven but are needed now.

We then learned the various things that a crown represents and the objects it contains. Each is significant.

We learned how we can lose, forfeit, or surrender our crowns through trauma, misinformation, fear, accusations, and several other reasons. Then, we learned how to retrieve lost crowns, have them placed upon us, and get them reactivated in our lives.

Many of the sons have lost their Crown of Sonship and, therefore, have lost their sense of sonship. That crown needs to be regained. Sometimes we were part of the problem. At other times we bought a lie from the enemy or people, and at other times, we allowed fear to dominate us in a situation, and our crown was stolen.

> *Do not let tough times make me seem distant from you. I am at hand—see my nearness, not my absence. And don't let temporal setbacks diminish your own authority either. Remember that you call the shots; you wear the crown. My crown endorses your crown. (Revelation 3:11, MIRROR)*

When we lose a crown, we lose the strength in the spirit that the crown we lost contained. We must regain *every* lost crown.

Later in our study on crowns, we were granted revelation regarding the seven false crowns placed upon the head of the dragon in Revelation 12:3. We read:

> *Then I witnessed in Heaven another significant event. I saw a large red dragon with seven heads and ten horns, with seven crowns on his heads. (NLT)*

We learned what those crowns were. This book will help you understand how they work together to destroy humanity and how we, as sons, can overcome. Enjoy the journey. It leads to victory!

———— ∞ ————

Chapter 1
The Goal of the Father

The goal of the Father is for the sons to recognize their place in His Kingdom fully and to step into a place of authority and govern. Having written over five books on the subject of Crowns, Heaven is still unpacking revelation regarding Crowns and how they are essential for the sons to grasp and walk in the authority of.

Our discovery began in early 2025 as Heaven began downloading revelation about the seven false crowns found in Revelation 12:3.

We need to look at the characteristics of these crowns and understand how they function together to bring destruction to people's lives. The listings in this book are somewhat different from other discussions about these crowns. They may help you have a fresh perspective on them. We will discuss twelve primary characteristics of each of the seven false crowns as well as the structures of these crowns. Some are more foundational than others, while some work in tandem. You will discover these details in this book.

We have also included the court cases under the heading "Prayers of Freedom" to bring freedom from these false crowns so that the sons can step into new arenas of freedom in their lives. We do not need to live powerless lives when the Father has made freedom and victorious living readily available to us, His sons.

We will be discussing the top 12 characteristics of each of the crowns as well as the structure of these crowns. The goal is to live as victorious sons. This book will help you in achieving that goal. Let's rise to the challenge.

———— ∞ ————

Chapter 2
The False Crown of Deception

The first crown we will discuss is the false Crown of Deception. It is foundational to the embrace of any of the other false crowns. The top twelve characteristics of the false Crown of Deception that you'll want to recognize are:

1. It has Self-Righteousness at Its Core. This crown is packed with all the 'selves'—self-righteousness, self-hatred, self-loathing, self-idolization, self-importance, and the particularly lethal self-justification, a toxic collection that feeds on itself. Often, one 'self-characteristic' feeds into another, creating a tangled mess that is challenging to disentangle, particularly if one is trying to break free without the Father's help.

2. It is Given to Delusions of Grandeur. People wearing this crown genuinely believe they're more right than everyone else. They experience an inflated sense of their importance and infallibility that disconnects them from reality. From reading the gospels, it is evident that the Pharisees, Sadducees, and teachers of the law wore this crown. Often, those who consider themselves biblical purists wear this crown as they think that their interpretation of Scripture is the only right one. Often, these individuals are steeped in dogma and have no trouble telling you how right they are about everything. They are opposed to revelation because it doesn't fit their mold of Scripture. Not surprisingly, wearers of this crown may feel they are on a special mission from God to straighten everyone else out. We have seen this repeatedly over the years.

3. It is Rooted in Pride. Pride is the foundation of this crown (and every other crown). It is the common denominator of all the false crowns. It's what makes someone think they're solely responsible for their success, and they refuse to acknowledge their need for humility or correction. In Psalm 100, we read that "It is He (God) that made us and not we ourselves." Those wearing this crown seem to forget that God is the Creator, not them. Pride will lead you to think you are more than you really are.

4. It is Disguised as Something Good. Here's the challenging part—this crown appears to be a good crown! It masquerades as wisdom, righteousness, or spiritual authority, making it incredibly deceptive. Often, those wearing this crown will interject themselves as the authority in an area and claim that they know the best way to do things. However,

Scripture teaches us that we are not **in** authority unless we are **under** authority, and the pride aspect of the false Crown of Deception will not allow them to submit to authority structures, as "they are above them" in their own eyes. If you are not *under* authority, you are not *in* authority!

5. It Comes Through Whispers and Accusations. The red dragon delivers this crown through subtle whispers that become accusations, creating offenses that divide people from truth and healthy relationships. It is vitally important that we arrest the whispers and utilize our soul realm angels to aid us in bringing every thought captive to the obedience of Christ. Whispers must be governed so they do not become accusations, for accusations can destroy lives.

6. It Creates an Unteachable Spirit. Those wearing this crown think they're infallible and certainly not to be questioned. They become resistant to correction, feedback, or different perspectives. Prophets often fall into this trap. *When you think you can't be wrong, you already are.* Pride, being the root of this false crown (and due to your insecurities), views everyone else as wrong and says, "you're not as enlightened as I am."

7. It Produces Restlessness and is Void of Peace. Unlike true crowns that bring peace, this false crown leaves its wearer constantly agitated, defensive, and without the peace that should guide our decisions. They are functioning from the Tree of the Knowledge of Good and Evil and not from the Tree of Life. They are constantly on defense and ready for the next confrontation. When pride is present, peace is not. Often turmoil is just under the surface.

8. It is Driven by the Need for Acceptance. Ironically, while appearing confident, those with this crown are desperately seeking acceptance and validation from others, making them vulnerable to manipulation and deception. A Crown of Deception opens the door for more deception.

9. It is Associated with an Orphan Mentality. This crown often sits on those who don't truly know their identity as beloved children, leading them to strive and perform for worth they already possess. They need acceptance but often drive away those who could help them the most.

10. It Refuses Truth and Correction. Any rejection of truth in one area opens the door for this crown. It creates a stubborn resistance to acknowledging wrong or accepting different viewpoints. It resists facing the fact that it might be wrong. They feel that rejection of something they say or believe is a rejection of the person, which is another aspect of an orphan mindset.

11. It Divides and Dominates. This crown's agenda is to separate people from truth and healthy relationships while establishing control and dominance over others. It is some of those healthy relationships that wearers of this crown are most in need of. The accusations cause division, and offense rears its ugly head. Often, the root of bitterness is involved in the lives of these persons. We will talk about the root of bitterness later in this book.

12. It Can be Generationally Transmitted. Perhaps most concerning, these false crowns can be passed down through family lines, affecting multiple generations until someone breaks the cycle through repentance and humility. The adage, "broken people break people," seems to be true with wearers of the false Crown of Deception. They can't heal others because they are so broken themselves. Often, they are so broken that they don't know they are broken. Pride won't let them see it in themselves. Everyone else is the problem. Knowing that these characteristics didn't start with you is somewhat freeing.

> *Our fathers sinned and are no more, but* ***we*** *bear their iniquities. (Lamentations 5:7)*

Someone in our ancestry likely embraced this false crown out of their brokenness. Repentance is key to freedom from this false crown.

Summary

The wonderful news is that recognizing these characteristics is the first step toward freedom! When we can identify this crown—whether on ourselves or others—we can choose the path of humility and truth that leads to genuine peace and authentic relationships. What I can identify, I can eliminate.

Narcissists are often wearers of this crown, as well as some of the other false crowns. A definition of narcissism is:

> *It's easy to describe someone who spends a bit too much time talking about her career or who never seems to doubt himself as a narcissist, but the trait is more complicated than that. Narcissism does not necessarily represent a surplus of self-esteem or of insecurity; more accurately, it encompasses a hunger for appreciation or admiration, a desire to be the center of attention, and an expectation of special treatment reflecting perceived higher status.... Many highly narcissistic people often readily admit to an awareness that they are more self-centered. A high level of narcissism, not surprisingly, can be damaging in romantic, familial, or professional relationships.*
>
> *Narcissism is characterized by a grandiose sense of self-importance, a lack of empathy for others, a need for excessive admiration, and the belief that one is unique and deserving of special treatment....*
>
> *Pathological narcissism, or narcissistic personality disorder, is rare: It affects an estimated 1 percent of the population, a prevalence that hasn't changed since clinicians started measuring it. The disorder is suspected when narcissistic traits impair a person's daily functioning. That dysfunction typically causes friction in relationships due to the pathological*

narcissist's lack of empathy. It may also manifest as antagonism, fueled by grandiosity and attention-seeking. In seeing themselves as superior, the pathological narcissist naturally views everyone else as inferior and may be intolerant of disagreement or questioning.[1]

Generational False Crowns

Sometimes, these false crowns are passed down from generation to generation. You want that false crown removed from your generational line. Repent for those in your generational line who embraced the Crown of Deception out of their brokenness, arrogance, and pride. Repent for any vestiges of pride, arrogance, or brokenness in your own life. Remove the inferior crown from your head and the crown on your generational line, and ask for the Crown of Humility in its place *and* the Crown of Righteousness.

Removal of a Generational False Crown

1. Repent for those in your generational line who have embraced the Crown of Deceit due to their brokenness, arrogance, and pride.

---

1. "Narcissism," Psychology Today, accessed February 5, 2026, https://www.psychologytoday.com/us/basics/narcissism.

2. Repent for any vestiges of pride, arrogance, or brokenness in your own life.
3. Remove the crown from your head and the crown on your generational line.
4. Ask for the Crown of Humility in its place, as well as the Crown of Righteousness.

The Crown That Looks Like Light:
Recognizing the False Crown of Deception

Pride goes before destruction, and a haughty spirit before a fall. (Proverbs 16:18)

The most dangerous deceptions are ones that look the most like truth. Here we're examining what may be the most pervasive of all false crowns—the Crown of Deception. This crown is particularly insidious because it doesn't present itself as obviously evil. Instead, it masquerades as wisdom, righteousness, and spiritual authority, making it one of the enemy's most effective tools.

Understanding this crown's structure isn't about becoming suspicious of everyone around us, it's about developing the discernment to recognize when pride and deception are operating—whether in ourselves or others—so we can pursue authentic humility and truth.

The Foundation: Pride as the Root System

Before we examine the specific structures, we need to understand that this crown is built on one foundational element: pride. Pride isn't just one characteristic among many—it's the common denominator of all false crowns and the root system that feeds every other deceptive element.

This pride creates the core delusion that we're "more than we really are" while refusing to acknowledge God as our Creator and sustainer. As Psalm 100:3 reminds us, "It is He that made us and not we ourselves," but this crown makes people forget this fundamental truth.

Structures of the False Crown of Deception

1. The Toxic Core: The Self-System

At the heart of this crown lies what can only be described as a toxic collection of "selves" that feed on each other:

- Self-righteousness (the primary element)
- Self-hatred and self-loathing
- Self-idolization and self-importance
- Self-justification (particularly lethal)

These characteristics create a "tangled mess" where one negative trait feeds into another, making it incredibly challenging to break free without divine assistance. It's a self-perpetuating system designed to keep people trapped in spiritual deception.

2. The Master Disguise: False Appearance Framework

Here's what makes this crown so dangerous—it appears to be good. It masquerades as wisdom, righteousness, or legitimate spiritual authority. People wearing this crown often position themselves as authorities in areas where they lack proper submission to established leadership.

This violates a fundamental kingdom principle: "If you are not under authority, you are not in authority." The crown's pride won't allow submission to proper authority structures because wearers believe they're "above" such accountability.

3. The Installation System: Whispers to Accusations

This crown is delivered through what's called the "Red Dragon Distribution Method"—starting with subtle whispers that gradually escalate to accusations. These whispers create offenses that systematically divide people from truth and healthy relationships.

This is why it's crucial to "bring every thought captive to the obedience of Christ" (2 Corinthians 10:5) with the help of spiritual discernment and accountability. Whispers that go ungoverned become accusations that can destroy lives and relationships.

4. The Defense Mechanism: Delusions of Grandeur and Unteachable Spirit

Once established, this crown creates powerful psychological defenses:

- Inflated sense of importance and personal infallibility
- Disconnection from reality
- Belief in being "more right than everyone else"
- Resistance to correction, feedback, or different perspectives

We see this pattern clearly in the Pharisees and Sadducees of Jesus's time, and unfortunately, in some who consider themselves "Biblical purists" today—those who believe their interpretation of Scripture is the only correct one and oppose any revelation that doesn't fit their theological framework.

5. The Identity Crisis: Orphan Mentality

This crown often operates in people who lack a true understanding of their identity as beloved children of God. This creates:

- Striving and performing for worth they already possess.
- Desperate need for acceptance while driving away those who could help most.
- Feeling that rejection of their ideas equals personal rejection.

This orphan mentality keeps people trapped in performance-based spirituality rather than resting in their secure identity in Christ.

6. The Relationship Destroyer: Division and Domination

The crown's agenda is clear: separate people from truth and healthy relationships while establishing control and dominance. It operates through:

- Creating accusations that cause division
- Establishing patterns of offense and bitterness
- Isolating people from the very relationships they need most

Ironically, those who wear this crown desperately need healthy relationships, yet their behavior systematically undermines the possibility of authentic community.

7. The Peace Killer: Restlessness and Spiritual Dysfunction

Unlike genuine spiritual authority that brings peace, this crown leaves its wearers:

- Constantly agitated and defensive
- Operating from the Tree of Knowledge of Good and Evil rather than the Tree of Life
- Ready for the next confrontation with turmoil just under the surface

When pride is present, peace cannot be. This restlessness is often a clear indicator that something is spiritually amiss.

8. The Vulnerability Creator: Desperate Need for Acceptance

Despite appearing confident, those wearing this crown are desperately seeking validation from others. This makes them vulnerable to manipulation and opens the door for additional deceptive influences. One Crown of Deception often leads to others.

9. The Truth Resistance System: Stubborn Rejection

Any rejection of truth in one area opens the door for this crown to gain influence. It creates stubborn resistance to acknowledging wrong or accepting different viewpoints because it cannot face the possibility of being incorrect.

10. The Generational Cycle: Inherited Brokenness

Perhaps most concerning is how this crown can be passed down through family lines, affecting multiple generations until someone breaks the cycle through repentance and humility. As Lamentations 5:7 states:

> *Our fathers sinned and are no more, but we bear their iniquities.*

The pattern of "broken people break people" continues until someone chooses to pursue healing and authentic humility.

Recognizing the Crown's Influence

How do we recognize when this crown might be operating—whether in ourselves or others?

Warning Signs:

- Inability to receive correction gracefully
- Positioning oneself as the final authority without proper accountability
- Creating division through accusations and offenses
- Desperate need for validation while appearing spiritually confident
- Operating in constant agitation rather than peace
- Viewing disagreement as personal attack
- Inability to acknowledge when wrong

The Path to Freedom

Breaking free from this crown requires:

Genuine Humility

Acknowledging that we don't have all the answers and desperately need both God and others in our lives.

Submission to Authority

Finding legitimate, accountable spiritual leadership and willingly placing ourselves under their care and correction.

Active Truth-Seeking

Welcoming correction and feedback rather than defending ourselves when confronted with uncomfortable truths.

Identity Reformation

Learning to rest in our identity as beloved children rather than performing for acceptance and validation.

Relationship Restoration

Pursuing authentic community and accountability rather than isolation and self-protection.

Generational Healing

If family patterns are involved, specifically repenting for generational pride and asking God to break inherited cycles.

A Word of Hope and Caution

Recognizing these patterns shouldn't lead to condemnation but to hope. The very fact that we can identify deceptive patterns means the light is beginning to shine in areas of darkness.

At the same time, we must approach this with humility, recognizing that we're all vulnerable to pride and deception. The moment we think we're immune to the Crown of Deception is likely the moment we become most susceptible to it.

Moving Forward in Authentic Authority

God desires to give His people genuine spiritual authority, but it looks nothing like the counterfeit this crown offers. True spiritual authority:

- Flows from intimacy with God, not performance for people
- Operates through service, not domination
- Functions in community, not isolation
- Brings peace, not constant agitation
- Welcomes accountability, not defensive independence

The Crown of Deception may be sophisticated in its operation, but it's no match for genuine humility, authentic community, and the transforming power of God's truth operating in our lives.

Remember, the goal isn't spiritual perfection—it's authentic relationship with God and others built on truth, humility, and love rather than pride, performance, and control.

God opposes the proud but shows favor to the humble. (James 4:6, NIV)

True spiritual maturity is measured not by how right we think we are, but by how quickly we're willing to acknowledge when we're wrong and how gracefully we receive correction.

Prayer for the Removal of the False Crown of Deception

Father, we ask to enter the realms of Heaven through Jesus. We invite the Seven Spirits of God, the angels, and our cloud of witnesses. We ask to enter the Court of Mercy.

We request that You bring into this Court everyone in our generations—on both our mother and father's side, as well as those related to us by blood, marriage, adoption, or civil or religious covenants—all the way to Your hand in the Garden and forward as far as it needs to go.

We request that the accuser of the brethren be brought into this Court. Your Honor, we agree with the adversary that we and our generations have picked up this false Crown of Deception through pride, arrogance, lies, delusions of grandeur, false humility, and through all the selves. We repent for every self-deception we have accepted and traded with. We repent for self-idolization, and we repent where we have been unteachable. We repent for self-promotion and self-striving instead of being led by Holy Spirit.

Father, we repent for deceiving others and for allowing this crown to rest upon their heads. We agree with the adversary that we have all been guilty of this. We repent for allowing the false mantle to fall on us and for being glad to wear it proudly.

We repent for hearing Your voice speaking to us to remove it, and instead we agreed to hang onto it tightly. We repent for not taking the keys of the Kingdom of Heaven and closing these doors, realms, gates, and bridges. We repent where You've allowed us to use the key of humility to close these doors forever, and instead we rebelled. We repent for the dishonor we brought upon ourselves, others, and You, Lord, for wearing this Crown of Deception, agreeing with delusions of grandeur, and thinking of ourselves more highly than we ought to.

We repent for being distracted by this Crown of Deception and allowing its deception to bring us further from the truth. We repent for being awestruck by the illusion of this crown. We repent for the throne, which is the altar of worship, where we have worshipped ourselves, worshipped what we've accomplished, and even worshipped the pain in our thoughts and minds.

We ask that the angels come and take this altar, this throne, and the idols upon it, which are all of our "self's." We repent for the use of this crown as well as every gray and black stone representing the "self's." We repent for where we have pride and present the crown, the throne, and the mantle to this court for judgment.

We ask that the angels bring every spirit associated with and assigned to this crown into the Court for judgment. We turn now to our generations, and we forgive, bless, and release you for participating in this crown. We forgive you for perpetuating it through the generations and for placing it upon the heads of others and we repent for where we have placed it upon the heads of others as well. We ask for the blood of Jesus. We ask for the full destruction of the crown, the throne, and the mantle.

We request that the stain of this crown that was left upon the heads of the sons be removed by the blood of Jesus, and we ask that it become white as snow. We request the mantles be rent in two and torn as we bow in this court before the Just Judge of the Universe. We bow in humility. We say, "Have mercy on us, Jesus." We ask that you walk through the timeline in our generations. Please deliver to us Your Crown of Righteousness. We agree that we have strayed because of these false, inferior crowns. We ask that you take our hand and bring our generations back to the truth. We ask for mercy and your righteous verdict on our behalf and those of our generations.

We receive your righteous verdict or further counsel, Your Honor.

> [If further counsel is advised, follow these instructions. Once you have received a righteous verdict, begin the following segment:]

With our righteous verdict in hand, we speak to the Earth. We speak to you—that every one of our generations who stepped upon you, even those related to us by blood, marriage, adoption, civil or religious covenant.

Earth, we have received a righteous verdict from the Courts of Heaven this day. We bless you to hear the word of the Lord. We bless you to swallow up the iniquity and the egregious sins of self-deception and wearing these crowns. Swallow up every word and deed that was done upon you. Swallow the innocent bloodshed, sexual sins, moving of the boundary stones, worship of ourselves, idol worship, occultic worship, theft—every sin under the sun that Jesus died for. We charge you to swallow it up and bless you to return to your original design. We bless you to see the governing sons and to begin blessing us. Begin pouring out your riches of abundance, of truth and life.

We request the blood of Jesus to cover every place this was done upon you or in you. We speak to the frequencies of the wind to blow away the evil, to the water to drown it, and to the fire to burn it. We speak to you to return to your original design as the Lord created you. The Earth is the Lord's, and its fullness belongs to the Lord.

We speak peace. We thank the Just Judge. We thank you, Jesus, the author and the finisher of our faith, for the Crowns of Righteousness and the Crown of Love that trump this inferior crown.

As governing sons, we pick up these superior crowns, place them upon our heads, and ask you to help us rule. We commission the angels to render these righteous verdicts in the spirit and the natural. We commission the angels to put this on record.

As sons, we call in the treasure that has been lost from the north, the south, the east, and the west in every age, realm, dimension, and time to fill the capacity of this section.

Thank You, Just Judge, for honoring us and trusting us with the responsibility of wearing these Crowns of Love and Righteousness. Thank you for helping us occupy the territory you assigned us. We don't take this lightly and we ask for supernatural assistance and help daily to govern well as your sons, in the name of Jesus.

We ask that all of this be done in time and out of time, and in every age, realm, and dimension, and that all spiritual debris, residue, and essences that were left behind by this inferior crown and the spirits that came with it be destroyed utterly. We thank you, Father, for what you did, Jesus, for giving us authority and dominion here.

———— ∞ ————

Chapter 3
The False Crown of Loathing

In the previous chapter, you learned about the false Crown of Deception. It is often the lead crown that seduces someone to embrace the next crown. Here are the top twelve characteristics of the false Crown of Loathing that you need to recognize and avoid:

1. It Demonstrates an Intense, All-Consuming Hatred. This crown represents the epitome of hatred—not just dislike, but a deep, intense loathing that goes to the very core. It's hatred at its most vicious and unrelenting level. It doesn't merely want to control others who don't view things as they do; it wants to see them destroyed.

2. It Abides in Complete Darkness and Is Void of Truth. This crown is described as "the blackest of black, void of light, void of truth." It represents absolute spiritual darkness that blocks out any possibility of understanding or compassion. It is so aligned with

Lucifer's mindset and motivations that it cannot be reasoned with. It is incredibly driven.

3. It Sits with Injustice as Its Foundation. The crown doesn't just tolerate injustice, it mandates it. It actively promotes and thrives on unfairness, cruelty, and wrongdoing as its operating system. It believes they are a law unto themselves and therefore whatever they want to do is permissible.

4. It Creates a False Sense of Belonging. Here's the deceptive part—this crown gives people a twisted sense of community and identity through shared hatred. It makes you feel like you belong to something, but it's completely false and destructive. When your common denominator with others is hatred of something or someone, your future cannot be good. They are usually not for anything but merely against something. They do not possess or offer a life-giving alternative.

5. It Has a Literal Spiritual Stench. Hatred and loathing create a spiritual foulness that affects everything around them. Hatred wants to dominate the atmosphere. This crown is not unlike the prior crowns we have discussed. It generates negative spiritual frequencies.

6. It Comes with a Throne of Wickedness. This isn't just a crown—it's a whole system that includes sitting on "a seat of wickedness and iniquity," positioning the wearer in darkness both now and eternally. We have seen this demonstrated in the United States with various "anti-ICE" riots. They are not just anti-ICE; they are basically anti-anything.

7. It Actively Opposes Love and Its Works. This crown doesn't just lack love—it actively loathes love, and anything that love produces. It will fight against kindness, compassion, and healing wherever it encounters them. Its desire to be hateful is nearly unfathomable. Still, your best weapon against this foul crown is love.

8. It Has an Enormous, Ferocious Appetite. The crown is described as consuming and ferocious, possessing an enormous appetite. It literally "eats you alive" and will consume even other dark entities—nothing satisfies its hunger for destruction. Like fire that never says, "I've had enough; I'll stop burning now," this crown is never satisfied. No amount of destruction is ever enough. With the destruction it brings, it doesn't care who is injured in the process.

9. It Begins with the Root of Bitterness. The pathway to this crown begins with bitterness, which often starts with offense, typically arising when we fail to govern the whispers and negative thoughts in our minds. The Crown of Deception shares this characteristic. Bitterness creates a justification to do whatever they want to destroy those they deem their enemies.

10. It Prevents Civil Discourse. You are wearing this crown if you cannot have a civil conversation with someone who disagrees with you politically or ideologically. It makes reasonable dialogue impossible. We have seen this manifest more in the last few years than ever before. The wearers of this crown are consumed with the belief that no opposing viewpoint can be allowed to stand.

11. It Makes You a Liar About Love. Scripture shows that if you claim to love God but hate others, you're a liar.[2] This crown creates fundamental dishonesty about your spiritual condition. Wearers of this crown cannot see their true condition. They are blinded to it.

12. It Leads to Spiritual Murder. Perhaps most sobering, the text references that *"whoever hates his brother is a murderer"*—this crown doesn't just harm relationships, it kills spiritual life and eternal hope. It kills relationships and wants to destroy opposing viewpoints. It often skips the three steps to the pattern of control, which are (1) they seek to **control** you. If that is unsuccessful, they go to step two. (2) They seek to **condemn** you. If that doesn't satisfy them, they progress to step three (3). They seek to **kill** you, either via character assassination or by actually killing you.

---

2. 1 John 4:20 If someone says, "I love God," and hates his brother, he is a liar; for he who does not love his brother whom he has seen, how can he love God whom he has not seen?

The Crown of Loathing doesn't hang around steps one or two very long. It goes straight for number three and seeks to kill you. Understanding the pattern can help you prepare for the challenges you may face with wearers of this crown.

Summary

Remember that this crown cannot be reasoned with. Unless Holy Spirit softens their heart, they will remain in this mindset of destruction. The encouraging truth is that Jesus died specifically so that no one should have to wear this crown! Recognition is the first step toward freedom. If you see any of these characteristics in yourself, remember that love is always the answer, and the fruits of the Spirit can replace this crown of darkness with something beautiful and life-giving.

The Darkest Crown: Understanding and Overcoming The False Crown of Loathing

Anyone who claims to be in the light but hates a brother or sister is still in the darkness. (1 John 2:9, NIV)

Today, we need to address what may be the darkest and most destructive of all false crowns, the Crown of Loathing. This isn't just about dislike or disagreement; this crown represents hatred at its most vicious and consuming level. While other false crowns deceive or manipulate, this one seeks complete destruction of anything that opposes it.

I want to approach this topic with both honesty about its dangers and hope about God's power to deliver anyone from its grip. No matter how deep the hatred or how dark the condition, there is always hope for redemption through Christ's love.

Why This Crown Is Uniquely Dangerous

The Crown of Loathing operates at the epitome of spiritual darkness. It's not content with control or influence—it wants complete annihilation of its perceived enemies. What makes it particularly dangerous is how it can masquerade as righteous anger or justified opposition, when in reality it's pure destruction masquerading as moral outrage.

This crown doesn't just harm the person wearing it; it creates a spiritual contamination that affects everyone in its vicinity. Understanding its structures can help us recognize its influence and find pathways to freedom.

Structures of the False Crown of Loathing

1. The Hatred Core: All-Consuming Destruction

At the center of this crown lies an intense, all-consuming hatred that goes far beyond normal human anger or disagreement. This isn't just dislike—it's a deep, vicious loathing that **seeks the complete destruction of those who think differently.**

Unlike healthy conviction that seeks to persuade or correct, this hatred doesn't want to change minds—it wants to eliminate the opposition entirely. It's hatred at its most unrelenting level.

2. The Darkness Void: Complete Absence of Light

This crown exists in what can only be described as "the blackest of black, void of light, void of truth." It represents absolute spiritual darkness that blocks out any possibility of understanding, compassion, or reason.

Those who wear this crown become so aligned with destructive motives that they cannot be reasoned with. They're extremely driven by dark purposes and completely unreachable through normal dialogue or appeal.

3. The Injustice Foundation: Wickedness as Its Operating System

Unlike crowns that merely tolerate wrong, this crown actively mandates injustice. It promotes and thrives on unfairness, cruelty, and wrongdoing as its core operating system.

Wearers believe they are a law unto themselves—whatever they want to do becomes permissible in their minds because their cause justifies any means necessary.

4. The False Unity: Community Built on Hatred

Here's where this crown becomes particularly deceptive—it creates a twisted sense of community and belonging through shared hatred. People often feel like they belong to something significant, but this is frequently completely false and destructive.

When your primary connection with others is hatred of something or someone, your future cannot be promising. These groups are typically not FOR anything positive—they're merely AGAINST others, offering no life-giving alternatives.

5. The Spiritual Contamination: Literal Stench

Hatred and loathing create what can only be described as a spiritual foulness that affects everything around them. This crown generates negative spiritual frequencies that contaminate the atmosphere wherever it operates.

The hatred wants to dominate not just conversations or situations, but <u>the entire spiritual environment</u>, making it difficult for others to experience peace, joy, or love in its presence.

6. The Wickedness Throne: Permanent Dark Authority

This crown is not just a temporary influence—it positions the wearer in spiritual darkness both now and potentially eternally.

We've seen this demonstrated in various movements where people aren't just opposed to specific policies or ideas, but seem to be fundamentally anti-everything that represents order, peace, or constructive solutions.

7. The Love Opposition: Active War Against Goodness

This crown doesn't simply lack love; it actively loathes love and everything love produces. It will fight against kindness, compassion, healing, and reconciliation wherever they are encountered.

The desire to be hateful becomes nearly unfathomable, making it difficult for observers to understand how someone could be so opposed to basic human kindness and decency.

8. The Consuming Fire: Insatiable Appetite for Destruction

Perhaps most terrifying is this crown's enormous, ferocious appetite for destruction. It literally "eats people alive" and will consume even other dark entities—nothing satisfies its hunger for annihilation.

Like fire that never says "enough," this crown is never satisfied with the destruction it leaves behind. It doesn't care who gets injured in the process as long as its targets are eliminated.

9. The Bitterness Pathway: The Road to Hatred

The pathway to this crown often begins with the root of bitterness, which typically arises from ungoverned whispers and negative thoughts in our minds.

Bitterness creates a sense of justification to do whatever is necessary to destroy those deemed enemies. What starts as hurt feelings can escalate into consuming hatred if left unchecked.

10. The Communication Killer: End of Civil Discourse

A clear warning sign of this crown's influence is the complete inability to have civil conversation with anyone who disagrees politically or ideologically. It makes reasonable dialogue impossible.

Wearers become consumed with the belief that no opposing viewpoint can be allowed to exist, let alone be discussed respectfully. This has become increasingly visible in our current cultural climate.

11. The Spiritual Deception: Lying About Love

Scripture teaches that if you claim to love God but hate others, you're a liar (1 John 4:20). This crown creates fundamental dishonesty about one's spiritual condition.

What's particularly tragic is that wearers cannot see their true condition—they're completely blinded to the contradiction between their claimed faith and their obvious hatred.

12. The Murder Mechanism: Spiritual and Sometimes Physical Death

Scripture warns that "*whoever hates his brother is a murderer*" (1 John 3:15). This crown doesn't just harm relationships—it kills spiritual life and eternal hope.

This crown typically skips the normal progression of control tactics:

- Step 1: Seek to control (skipped quickly)
- Step 2: Seek to condemn (skipped quickly)
- Step 3: Seek to kill (goes straight here)

Whether through character assassination or actual violence, this crown seeks immediate destruction rather than influence or correction.

Recognizing the Warning Signs

How do you know if you or someone you care about might be under this crown's influence?

- **Inability to have a respectful dialogue** with those who disagree
- **Dehumanizing language** toward opponents or "enemies."
- **Justifying cruel or unfair treatment** of others

- **Finding identity primarily in opposition** rather than a positive purpose
- **Experiencing satisfaction** when "enemies" suffer setbacks or harm
- **Isolation from people** who don't share your hatred
- **Spiritual pride** that claims divine justification for destructive behavior

The Path to Freedom

If you recognize this crown's influence, here's the pathway to freedom:

1. Acknowledge the Hatred

The first step is honest recognition that what you're experiencing isn't righteous anger—it's consuming hatred that's destroying your spiritual life.

2. Repent for Bitterness

Trace back to where the bitterness began and specifically repent for allowing offense to grow into hatred.

3. Choose Forgiveness

This doesn't mean agreeing with those who hurt you but releasing your right to revenge and trusting God with justice.

4. Seek Reconciliation Where Possible

Not all relationships can be restored, but where possible, pursue peace and understanding.

5. Find Positive Purpose

Instead of being primarily against things, discover what you're called to be FOR in God's kingdom.

6. Practice Love as Warfare

The most effective weapon against this crown is active, intentional love—even toward those who oppose you.

A Word of Hope

I know this might seem overwhelming, especially if you recognize some of these patterns in yourself or others. But here's what I want you to remember: no one is beyond the reach of God's love and transforming power.

I've seen people completely consumed by hatred find freedom through Christ's love. I've witnessed the hardest hearts soften when touched by genuine compassion. The darkness of this crown is real, but the light of Christ is more powerful.

For Those Affected by Others' Hatred

If you're dealing with someone wearing this crown, remember:

- **Don't take their hatred personally**—it's the crown speaking, not their true identity.
- **Maintain your own spiritual health**—don't let their darkness contaminate your light.
- **Pray for their deliverance**—they're in spiritual bondage and need freedom.
- **Set appropriate boundaries**—love doesn't mean accepting abuse.
- **Seek support**—you don't have to face this alone.

The Power of Love Over Hatred

Here's the beautiful truth: love is always stronger than hatred. Light always overcomes darkness. The Crown of Loathing may be the darkest of all false crowns, but it cannot withstand the persistent, patient, powerful love of Christ working through His people.

Your best weapon against this crown—whether in yourself or others—is love. Not passive tolerance, but active, intentional, Christ-centered love that refuses to be overcome by evil and instead overcomes evil with good.[3]

---

3. Romans 12:21

Moving Forward

As we close, I want to encourage you to examine your own heart honestly. Are there areas of bitterness, offense, or growing hatred that need to be addressed before they develop into something more dangerous?

At the same time, don't live in fear of this crown. Live in the confidence that God's love in you is more powerful than any hatred around you. You were created to be a light in the darkness, not to be overcome by it.

The Crown of Loathing may represent the epitome of spiritual darkness, but you serve the One who is the Light of the World. In His light, even the deepest darkness must flee.

But I tell you, love your enemies and pray for those who persecute you, that you may be children of your Father in heaven. (Matthew 5:44-45, NIV)

Love isn't just the answer to hatred—it's the only answer that works. Choose love, even when it's difficult. Especially when it's difficult.

Removal of the Crown of Loathing

1. Do a self-check first.
2. Repent for where we have embraced the Crown of Loathing out of hatred and the root of bitterness.

3. Repent for embracing offense.
4. Repent for every vestige of hatred, disrespect, dishonor, and lying in your life.
5. Remove the false crown from your head.
6. Request a cleansing of your realms from the vestiges of this false crown.
7. Ask for the Crown of Love for yourself.
8. Pray in the Spirit for yourself.

Interceding for Those Captured by This False Crown

1. Repent for where the person has embraced the Crown of Loathing out of hatred and the root of bitterness.
2. Repent for them embracing offense.
3. Repent for every vestige of hatred, disrespect, dishonor, and lying in their life.
4. Remove the false crown from their head.
5. Request a cleansing of their realms from the vestiges of this false crown.
6. Ask for the Crown of Love to be placed upon them.
7. Pray in the Spirit for them.

Prayer for Removal of the False Crown of Loathing

Father, we ask to step into the Court of Mercy to receive mercy in our time of need. We request the accuser of the brethren to be brought in, as well as our generations, those related to us by blood, marriage, adoption, civil or religious covenant, all the way to Your hand in the Garden and as far forward as it needs to go.

We come to You, and we repent for embracing the Crown of Loathing out of hatred and the root of bitterness. We repent for embracing offense, and we repent for every vestige of hatred, disrespect, dishonor, and lying in our own lives.

We repent where we have ever loathed anyone or anything in our generations. We repent where we have allowed, agreed with, or perpetuated the spirit of antichrist, but also where those who are or were anti-God allowed this inferior crown to bring an atheistic mentality. We repent for cooperating with that. We repent for our hatred of the Father and those who are His. We repent for engaging in the stench of these sins. We repent for sitting in a league with injustice, promoting injustice, and being unjust. We repent for mandating the wickedness of injustice.

We repent for being void of truth. We repent for agreeing with, being a part of, and loving the sense of belonging by wearing this inferior crown. We repent for sitting on the throne of loathing with its seat of wickedness and iniquity. We repent for the great error of wearing this crown. We repent for believing the false acceptance, the pride, and the belief that we do not have to love you or anyone else, only ourselves. Please forgive us. We repent for loathing love. We repent for not accepting your love and for not loving others or even ourselves.

Father, forgive us and our generations, those who were atheists, those who loathed the Word of God, the truth around it, and those who had bitterness in their hearts; we repent. We repent for the utter hatred of anything that presented itself from you or from others that were or carried the embodiment of Your love or what it would bring. We repent for having an appetite for loathing and for hating you, God and man.

We ask for the angels to go through time, on behalf of ourselves and our generations, to remove the crowns of loathing and destroy them.

We ask the angels to remove the Crowns of Loathing placed upon our family's heads, of those who don't trust or believe, for it came from an iniquitous generation. We ask that the throne be destroyed, the seat of wickedness be destroyed, and iniquity be forever vanquished, banished, and removed forevermore from us and our generations. We repent for being a part of consuming the innocent and taking innocence away from others because of wearing this inferior crown. We repent for being part of others losing their Superior Crowns, for removing them, for their crowns becoming lost.

Jesus, we ask for your blood to cover us and for those crowns to be removed from our children, our grandchildren, our mothers, our fathers, our sisters, our brothers, our friends, and our neighbors. We speak that it must bow to the Superior Crown of King Jesus and the crowns we wear—The Crown of Sonship and the Crown of Love, in Jesus' name.

Righteous Judge, we ask for your verdict or further counsel.

> [If further counsel is advised, follow these instructions. Once you have received a righteous verdict, begin the following segment:]

We speak to the Earth on which every one of our generations stepped, including those related to us by blood, marriage, adoption, civil or religious covenant.

Earth, we have received a righteous verdict from the Courts of Heaven this day. We bless you to hear the word of the Lord. We bless you to swallow up the iniquity and the egregious sins of self-deception and the wearing of these inferior crowns. Swallow up every word and deed that was done upon you. Swallow the innocent bloodshed, sexual sins, moving of the boundary stones, worship of ourselves, idol worship, occultic worship, theft—every sin under the sun that Jesus died for. We charge you to swallow it up and bless you to your original design. We bless you to see the governing sons and to begin blessing us. Begin pouring out your riches of abundance of truth and life.

We request the blood of Jesus to cover every place this was done upon you or in you. We speak to the frequencies of the wind to blow away the evil, to the water to drown it, and to the fire to burn it. We speak to you to return to your original design as the Lord had created you. The Earth is the Lord's, and its fullness belongs to the Lord.

We speak peace. We thank the Just Judge. We thank you, Jesus, the author and the finisher of our faith, for the Crowns of Righteousness and the Crown of Love that trump this inferior crown.

As governing sons, we pick up these Superior Crowns, place them upon our heads, and ask you to help us rule. We commission the angels to render these righteous verdicts in the spirit and the natural. We commission the angels to put this on record.

Thank you, Just Judge, for honoring us and trusting us with the responsibility of wearing these Crowns of Love and Righteousness. Thank you for helping us occupy the territory you assigned us. We don't take this lightly and ask for supernatural assistance and help daily to govern well as your sons, in the name of Jesus.

As a son, we call in the treasure that has been lost from the north, the south, the east, and the west in every age, realm, dimension, and time to fill the capacity of this section.

Thank you, Just Judge, for honoring us and trusting us with the responsibility of wearing these Crowns of Love and Righteousness. Thank you for helping us occupy the territory you assigned us. We don't take this lightly, and we ask for supernatural assistance and help daily to govern well as your sons, in the name of Jesus.

We ask that all of this be done in time and out of time, and in every age, realm, and dimension, and that all of the spiritual debris, residue, and essences that were left behind by this inferior crown and the spirits that came with it be destroyed utterly. We thank you, Father, for what you did, Jesus, for giving us authority and dominion here.

———— ∞ ————

Chapter 4

The False Crown of Fear

The top 12 characteristics of the false Crown of Fear that you need to recognize and guard against:

1. It is Superior Among Inferior Crowns. This crown is described as "superior in its inferiority," meaning it's particularly powerful and dangerous compared to other false crowns. It operates with exceptional strength and influence. It undergirds the other false crowns and maintains dominance through fear.

2. It Affects Both Believers and Unbelievers. Unlike some spiritual issues that primarily target one group, this crown doesn't discriminate—it operates quite strongly in both those who believe and those who don't, making everyone vulnerable. As sons, we must choose not to cooperate with fear at any time, on any level, about anything, in any place. It must be a firm decision.

3. It Comes with Multiple Demonic Entities. When this crown is placed on someone's head, it doesn't come alone. Many demonic entities are released into the person's life, as if they're entering through a back door with an entire entourage of darkness. Fear will introduce terror into your life. You live in terror when you consult fear before making a decision or taking action. For example, you won't do something because you fear something else will occur.

4. It Creates a Throne of Negativity. This crown opens up a throne, and from that position of authority, negative things begin pouring out, encircling the person's head and trying to manifest around, in, and through their mind. It is essential to utilize your soul-realm angels to help capture every negative thought and bring it into captivity.

5. It Distorts Mental and Heart Function. The crown distorts both the mind and the heart, affecting your ability to think clearly and feel appropriately. It corrupts your emotional and mental processing. Fear has many effects on a person, particularly on the heart.

6. It Rules Over Other Inferior Crowns. This crown holds a hierarchical position, governing and controlling many other false crowns, making it a master controller in the kingdom of darkness.

7. It is Often Trauma-Induced. Many people have this crown thrust upon them through traumatic experiences. It's not always a choice—sometimes it's forced upon people through painful circumstances beyond their control. If you have ever been involved in an automobile accident, you may have had a brief moment when you could embrace fear or reject it. At the moment of embrace, a crown of fear was placed upon your head and began its evil work of introducing other fears into your life.

8. It Blocks Heavenly Reception. When you're wearing this crown, you'll have trouble receiving from Heaven. It creates interference with your spiritual connection and ability to hear from God. Fear suggests things that are not in keeping with the heart of the Father.

9. It Can Be Generational. Fear doesn't just affect individuals—it can be passed down through previous generations, meaning you might inherit this burden from family patterns and ancestral issues.

10. It Acts as a Master Manipulator. This crown is described as a master manipulator that creates strongholds. It's cunning, strategic, and knows precisely how to maintain control once it gains a foothold. We must recognize when it is at work and how it seeks to further its influence in your life and control you.

11. It Embeds Itself Like an Inverted Crown. Rather than sitting on top of the head like a regular crown, this one digs into the person's head, piercing it as if the crown were inverted. It doesn't just rest—it penetrates and becomes embedded. Picture the points of a crown when it is inverted, not unlike the crown of thorns that pierced Jesus' scalp when placed on His head.

12. It Blocks Revelation and Spiritual Flow. For those called to be governing sons and daughters, this crown is particularly destructive because it distorts your ability to receive and flow in revelation—the very thing you need to operate in your calling. It suggests all sorts of things to you, trying to get you to be afraid to receive revelation, saying it will make others think poorly of you. It will harm your standing among your family or friends. It suggests that you will be rejected and ridiculed...all to get you to shut down the reception of revelation into your life.

Summary

The beautiful truth is that God has not given us a spirit of fear, but of power, love, and a sound mind! When you recognize these characteristics in yourself or others, remember that this crown can be removed and replaced with the authentic authority and peace that comes from Heaven. You have the power to reject this crown and choose the freedom that's rightfully yours!

This crown, in particular, is often passed down through the generations. Repentance for its embrace by your generations will be necessary to begin the steps to freedom.

Structures of the False Crown of Fear

Breaking Free from the False Crown of Fear

For God has not given us a spirit of fear, but of power and of love and of a sound mind. (2 Timothy 1:7)

Fear is one of the enemy's most effective weapons, and for good reason—it affects everyone. Believers and unbelievers alike face its grip, making it one of the most universal spiritual battles we encounter. Today, we're examining what may be the most controlling of all false crowns: the false Crown of Fear.

Understanding this crown isn't about becoming fearful of fear itself. Rather, it's about recognizing its tactics so we can resist effectively, walk in freedom, and help others break free from its paralyzing grip.

The Master Controller

Here's something you need to understand: the Crown of Fear isn't just another spiritual problem—it's described as "superior in its inferiority," meaning it's exceptionally powerful and dangerous compared to other false crowns. It functions as the master controller in the kingdom of darkness, actually undergirding and maintaining dominance over other false crowns.

When fear gains a foothold in your life, it creates the perfect environment for other deceptions to take root. It's like the foundation upon which the enemy builds other spiritual strongholds.

The Twelve Structures of Control

1. The Hierarchy of Control: Superior Dominance

This crown holds a unique hierarchical position, governing and controlling many other false crowns. It operates with exceptional strength and influence, making it a master controller that enables other spiritual bondages to function more effectively.

When you break free from fear, you'll often find that other spiritual struggles lose their power as well.

2. The Universal Target: No One Is Immune

Unlike some spiritual issues that primarily target specific groups, this crown doesn't discriminate. It operates strongly in both believers and unbelievers, making absolutely everyone vulnerable to its influence.

This means that as sons and daughters of God, we must make a firm, active decision not to cooperate with fear at any time, on any level, about anything, in any place. This isn't a passive hope—it's an intentional choice we must make daily.

3. The Demonic Network: Multiple Entity System

When this crown is placed on someone's head, it doesn't come alone. Many demonic entities are released into that person's life, entering through what's described as a "back door" with a whole entourage of darkness.

Fear introduces terror into your life. You begin living in terror when you consult fear before making decisions or taking action. "I won't do that because I'm afraid something bad will happen" becomes your default response to life's opportunities and challenges.

4. The Command Center: Throne of Negativity

This crown opens up a throne—a position of authority from which negative things begin pouring out, encircling your head and trying to manifest around, in, and through your mind.

This is why it's essential to utilize your soul-realm angels to help capture every negative thought and bring it into captivity to Christ. The battle for your mind is real, and you need heavenly assistance to win it.

5. The Distortion System: Mental and Heart Corruption

The crown distorts both mind and heart, impairing your ability to think clearly and feel appropriately. It corrupts your emotional and mental processing in ways that seem entirely natural for you.

Fear has myriad effects on a person, particularly on the heart. Anxiety, panic attacks, and stress-related health issues often have their roots in this spiritual crown.

6. The Master Position: Ruling Over Other Crowns

This crown's hierarchical position means it governs and controls many other false crowns. It's not just about being afraid; it's about how fear enables pride, deception, bitterness, and other spiritual problems to gain ground in your life.

Breaking the Crown of Fear often results in breakthrough in multiple areas simultaneously.

7. The Entry Point: Trauma-Induced Installation

Many people have this crown thrust upon them through traumatic experiences. It's not always a choice—sometimes it's forced upon people through painful circumstances beyond their control.

Think about it: if you've ever been in an automobile accident, there was a brief moment when you could either embrace fear or reject it. At the moment of embrace, a crown of fear was placed upon your head and began its evil work of introducing other fears into your life.

8. The Barrier: Blocking Heavenly Reception

When you're wearing this crown, you'll have trouble receiving from Heaven. It creates interference with your spiritual connection and ability to hear from God clearly.

Fear suggests things that are not in keeping with the heart of the Father. It distorts your understanding of God's character and makes you question His goodness, timing, and intentions.

9. The Legacy: Generational Transmission

Fear doesn't just affect individuals—it can be passed down through previous generations. You might inherit this burden from family patterns and ancestral issues.

Have you noticed that certain fears run in your family? That's not a coincidence—it's generational transmission that needs to be broken through repentance and spiritual authority.

10. The Strategy: Master Manipulation

This crown is a master manipulator that creates strongholds. It's cunning, strategic, and knows precisely how to maintain control once it gains a foothold in your life.

We must recognize when it's at work and how it seeks to further its influence and control. Fear rarely announces itself; instead, it works through subtle suggestions and "what if" scenarios.

11. The Physical Reality: Inverted Crown Installation

Rather than sitting on top of the head like a regular crown, this one digs into the person's head, piercing it as if the crown were inverted. It doesn't just rest—it penetrates and becomes embedded.

Picture the points on a crown when inverted, not unlike the crown of thorns that pierced Jesus's scalp when placed on His head. This physical embedding represents how fear creates lasting patterns that require intentional spiritual warfare to remove.

12. The Calling Killer: Blocking Revelation and Spiritual Flow

For those called to be governing sons and daughters, this crown is particularly destructive because it distorts your ability to receive and flow in revelation—the very thing you need to operate in your calling.

Fear suggests all sorts of things to you:

- "If you receive this revelation, others will think poorly of you."
- "This will harm your standing with family or friends."
- "You'll be rejected and ridiculed."

All these suggestions are designed to shut down the reception of revelation into your life and prevent you from fulfilling your divine purpose.

Recognizing Fear's Grip

How do you know if this crown has an influence on your life?

- **You consult fear** rather than seeking God's wisdom before making decisions.
- **You avoid opportunities** because of potential negative outcomes.
- **You can't receive spiritual gifts or pursue a calling** due to fear of others' opinions.
- **You experience physical symptoms** like heart palpitations or anxiety.
- **You isolate from the community** to avoid judgment or rejection.
- **You overthink everything,** constantly running through "what if" scenarios.
- **You struggle to hear God's voice** or receive from Heaven.

The Path to Freedom

Here's the beautiful truth: God has not given us a spirit of fear, but of power, love, and a sound mind! When you recognize these characteristics in yourself or others, remember that this crown can be removed and replaced with the authentic authority and peace that comes from Heaven.

Step 1: Recognize and Reject

Make a firm decision not to cooperate with fear at any level. Recognize when fear is speaking and actively reject its suggestions.

Step 2: Address Generational Patterns

This crown is often passed down through generational lines. Repentance for ancestors' embrace is necessary to begin the steps toward freedom. Stand in your authority and break generational fear patterns over your bloodline.

Step 3: Engage Spiritual Warfare

Utilize your soul realm angels to capture negative thoughts. Take every thought captive to the obedience of Christ. This isn't passive—it's active spiritual warfare.

Step 4: Receive Truth

Replace fear's lies with God's truth. When fear says you'll be rejected, God says you're accepted. When fear says you'll fail, God says you're equipped. When fear says you're alone, God says He'll never leave you.

Step 5: Choose Action Despite Fear

Courage isn't the absence of fear—it's action in the presence of fear. Take one step forward while trusting God with the outcome.

Living in Freedom

You have the power to reject this crown and choose the freedom that's rightfully yours! The Crown of Fear may be a master controller, but it's no match for the perfect love of your Heavenly Father.

Remember what Scripture tells us: *"Perfect love casts out fear"* (1 John 4:18). When you truly understand how much you're loved and how completely you're protected in Christ, fear loses its power to control your decisions and destiny.

Don't let fear steal another day, another opportunity, or another moment of peace. You were created to walk in power, love, and a sound mind. That's not just a nice thought—it's your spiritual birthright in Christ.

Stand up, shake off that inverted crown, and step into the freedom that's already yours!

Fear is a liar. Love is the truth. Choose love, choose courage, choose freedom—choose the life God always intended for you.

Why This Crown Rules Over Others

The Crown of Fear holds a unique position in the kingdom of darkness—it's described as "superior in its inferiority," meaning it's exceptionally powerful among false crowns. It functions as the master controller that rules over other inferior crowns and provides foundational support for other deceptive systems.

This crown's power lies in its ability to paralyze, isolate, and systematically shut down our spiritual receptivity. When fear gains control, it creates the perfect environment for other deceptions to take root.

The Twelve Control Mechanisms

1. The Hierarchy of Control: Superior Dominance

This crown operates as the master controller in the enemy's kingdom, ruling over other false crowns and providing the foundational fear that enables other deceptive systems to function effectively.

When fear takes root, it creates vulnerability to pride (as we try to protect ourselves), deception (as we lose clarity of thought) and other spiritual bondages. Fear is often the gateway crown that opens the door for others.

2. The Physical Reality: Inverted Crown Installation

Unlike crowns that sit on top of the head, this one embeds itself like an inverted crown, with points that dig into and pierce the head. This creates a permanent embedding that's difficult to remove—similar to how the crown of thorns pierced Jesus's scalp.

This physical embedding represents how fear doesn't just influence us temporarily; it creates lasting patterns of thought and behavior that require intentional spiritual warfare to overcome.

3. The Universal Target: No One Is Exempt

This crown affects both believers and unbelievers equally. No one has natural immunity to fear, which makes it universally dangerous. It requires a firm decision not to cooperate with fear at any level, in any circumstance.

The universality of fear means we must all actively choose courage rather than passively hoping we won't be afraid. Faith isn't the absence of fear—it's the decision to trust God despite fear's presence.

4. The Demonic Network: Multiple Entity System

When this crown is placed, it doesn't come alone. Many demonic entities enter through what's described as a "back door," bringing a whole entourage of darkness that escalates basic fear into terror.

This explains why some fears seem disproportionate to their triggers—they're not just natural anxiety but spiritual attacks designed to create terror that paralyzes decision-making and spiritual growth.

5. The Command Center: Throne of Negativity

This crown creates its own throne from which to operate, establishing a position of authority for negative manifestation. It pours out negative thoughts that encircle the head, specifically targeting the mind for maximum impact.

When fear establishes a throne in our thinking, it becomes the lens through which we interpret everything—turning even neutral circumstances into threats and blocking our ability to see God's goodness and faithfulness.

6. The Interference System: Mental and Spiritual Corruption

This crown systematically distorts mental function, corrupts heart responses, and interferes with emotional processing. It also creates physical effects on the heart and body while blocking our ability to receive from Heaven.

Fear doesn't just affect our emotions—it impacts our entire being, making it difficult to think clearly, feel appropriately, or connect spiritually with God and others.

7. The Entry Points: Trauma and Generational Transmission

This crown often enters through traumatic experiences where there's a brief moment of decision to embrace or reject fear. Automobile accidents and similar traumas become entry points where fear can take hold.

Additionally, it can be passed down through generational patterns, creating inherited vulnerabilities that affect multiple generations until someone breaks the cycle through spiritual warfare and faith.

8. The Control Strategy: Master Manipulation

Once established, this crown operates as a master manipulator, creating strongholds through cunning strategy. It's strategic and precise in maintaining control, knowing exactly how to maintain its foothold and expand its influence.

Fear rarely operates obviously—it works through subtle suggestions, "what if" scenarios, and gradual erosion of confidence in God's protection and provision.

9. The Decision Paralysis: Terror-Based Living

This crown creates a lifestyle where fear is consulted before every action. People begin living in terror, preventing action through fear of consequences and paralyzing the decision-making process entirely.

When we start asking fear's opinion before making decisions, we've given it authority over our lives that belongs only to God and His wisdom.

10. The Calling Killer: Revelation Blocking

This crown is particularly destructive for those called to be governing sons and daughters because it distorts the ability to receive revelation and blocks the fulfillment of their calling. It suggests fears about receiving from God:

- Fear that others will think poorly of you.
- Fear of harming your standing with family or friends.
- Fear of rejection and ridicule.

These fears effectively shut down our ability to receive the revelation we need to fulfill our divine purpose.

11. The Battle Requirement: Angelic Assistance Needed

Breaking free from this crown requires utilizing soul realm angels to capture negative thoughts and bring them into captivity to Christ. Active spiritual warfare and angelic assistance are necessary for effective thought management.

This isn't something we can overcome through willpower alone—it requires engaging spiritual resources and heavenly assistance to capture and redirect our thought patterns.

12. The Escalation System: Fear Multiplication

This crown introduces terror beyond basic fear, multiplying fears so that one fear leads to many. It creates a fear of receiving spiritual gifts and a calling, building strongholds that resist breakthroughs.

Fear has a reproductive quality—one fear creates others, eventually creating a fortress of terror that seems impossible to overcome without divine intervention.

Recognizing Fear's Control

How do you know if this crown has gained influence in your life?

- **Consulting fear before making decisions** rather than seeking God's wisdom.
- **Avoiding opportunities** because of potential negative outcomes.
- **Inability to receive spiritual gifts** or pursue a calling due to fear of others' opinions.
- **Physical symptoms** like heart palpitations, anxiety, or panic in spiritual situations.
- **Isolation from the spiritual community** to avoid judgment or rejection.
- **Overthinking and "what if" scenarios** that prevent forward movement.
- **Feeling like God can't be trusted** in difficult circumstances.

The Biblical Response to Fear

Scripture gives us clear strategies for overcoming fear:

Choose Faith Over Fear

Fear not, for I am with you; be not dismayed, for I am your God; I will strengthen you, yes, I will help you, I will uphold you with My righteous right hand. (Isaiah 41:10)

Take Thoughts Captive

We demolish arguments and every pretension that sets itself up against the knowledge of God, and we take captive every thought to make it obedient to Christ. (2 Corinthians 10:5, NIV)

Perfect Love Casts Out Fear

There is no fear in love. But perfect love drives out fear, because fear has to do with punishment. The one who fears is not made perfect in love. (1 John 4:18, NIV)

Focus on God's Faithfulness

When I am afraid, I put my trust in you. In God, whose word I praise—in God I trust and am not afraid. (Psalm 56:3-4, NIV)

Breaking Free from the Crown of Fear

Here are practical steps for overcoming fear's control:

1. Recognize Fear's Voice

Learn to distinguish between wisdom (which considers risks while trusting God) and fear (which assumes the worst and paralyzes action).

2. Speak Truth Over Fear

When fear suggests lies about God's character or your future, counter with biblical truth about His faithfulness and protection.

3. Take Action Despite Fear

Courage isn't the absence of fear—it's action in the presence of fear. Take one step forward while trusting God with the outcome.

4. Engage Spiritual Warfare

Ask for angelic assistance in capturing fearful thoughts and replacing them with faith-filled thinking.

5. Build Faith Through God's Word

"Faith comes by hearing, and hearing by the word of God" (Romans 10:17). Regular time in Scripture builds faith that displaces fear.

6. Seek Community Support

Fear isolates, but community provides strength, encouragement, and accountability for walking in courage.

7. Address Generational Patterns

If fear has been a family pattern, specifically pray for generational healing and breaking of inherited fear patterns.

Living in Freedom

The Crown of Fear may be a master controller, but it's no match for the perfect love of our heavenly Father. When we truly understand how much we're loved and how completely we're protected in Christ, fear loses its power to control our decisions and destiny.

Remember that God has not given you a spirit of fear, but of power, love, and a sound mind (2 Timothy 1:7). You were created to walk in courage, receive revelation, and fulfill your calling without fear's interference.

The enemy may use fear as his master weapon, but we serve the One who conquered every fear through His death and resurrection. In Him, we can live courageously, receive boldly, and walk confidently in the destiny He has prepared for us.

> *Be strong and courageous! Do not be afraid or discouraged. For the Lord your God is with you wherever you go. (Joshua 1:9, NIV)*

Perfect love casts out fear. When we truly know how loved we are, fear loses its power to control us.

Labeling

The false Crown of Loathing relies on false labels.

The structure of the false Crown of Loathing is built upon labels, lies, and loathing.

With the false Crown of Loathing, you don't reason; you react.

You aren't objective; you obfuscate ("to throw into shadow"—to be evasive, unclear, or confusing). One label will follow another. Listed are commonly used labels and their actual definition:

Racist: of, relating to, or characterized by racism: such as having, reflecting, or fostering the belief that race is a fundamental determinant of human traits and capacities and that racial differences produce an inherent superiority of a particular race.

Homophobe: a person characterized by homophobia—discrimination against, aversion to, or fear of homosexuality or gay people.

Nazi: a member of a German fascist party controlling Germany from 1933 to 1945 under Adolf Hitler; one who espouses the beliefs and policies of the German Nazis; one who is likened to a German Nazi: a **harshly domineering**, **dictatorial**, or **intolerant person.**

Fascist: a populist political philosophy, movement, or regime (such as that of the *Fascisti*) that exalts nation and often race above the individual, that is associated with a centralized autocratic government headed by a dictatorial leader, and that is characterized by severe economic and social regimentation and by **forcible suppression of opposition.**

Misogynist: a person who hates or discriminates against women; a misogynistic person; feeling, showing, or characterized by hatred of or prejudice against women.

Bigot: a person who is obstinately or intolerantly devoted to his or her own opinions and prejudices; especially: one who regards or treats the members of a group (such as a racial or ethnic group) with hatred and intolerance.

Labels are accusations

The enemy wants the accusations untreated to become false verdicts because:

Accusations affect behavior.

False Verdicts DICTATE behavior.

Prayer for Removal of the False Crown of Fear

Lord, we ask to step into Your Court of Mercy to receive mercy in our time of need. We ask that our generations be brought into this Court and those related to us by blood, marriage, adoption, civil or religious covenant, to Your hand in the Garden and forward as far as it needs to go.

Lord, I present to You ourselves and our generations—every one of us who ever wore this inferior crown, who willingly took this Crown of Fear, who even distributed it to other people in our family and our generations, and even those outside of our generations where we instilled fear, presented fear, were a part of fear, or perpetuated fear throughout the generational line, or where we have accepted it, bent our knee to it, or even relished in it, or relished in it in others. Forgive us, Lord; we repent. I ask for the blood of Jesus to be applied to this.

We are requesting that this inferior crown be removed from us and our generational line, as it pierced our heads. We ask that the angels remove this crown, even though it is not easily taken off, along with every binding and every structure that would keep it upon the heads of the sons, and that the crown be taken off and destroyed.

We ask that the Superior Crown of Love be placed upon our heads to heal any woundedness and begin to mend our minds and mend the places of woundedness.

We ask that the technology of the Crowns of Sonship that we wear in this new day would infiltrate and destroy the technology of the Crown of Fear, and that the nanotechnology of Jesus—of His love (for He has not given us the spirit of fear, but of power)—and the power and the dominion of the Superior Crown crush and destroy the inferior Crown of Fear.

The Father has not given us the spirit of fear but of love, and that love is the Supreme Crown over this inferior crown. As the Crown of a Sound Mind is placed upon our heads, may it heal every wound of the mind, and may the poison that came with that inferior Crown of Fear be drawn up out of us as we are made new.

We commission the angels to clean up the spiritual debris, residue, and essences that the spirit of fear has left behind, and we receive the Crown of Superiority from Jesus, the Crown of Love, the Crown of Power, the dominion over this, and the Crown of a Sound Mind. Thank You, Lord.

We come out of agreement with every superiority of this inferior crown. We are not in agreement with it. Where we and our generations agreed, and where we were lied to, and we believed that there was nothing we could do because we were so gripped by fear; that is a lie. We come out of agreement with the lie of this inferior Crown of Fear. We ask for the cancellation and annulment of these lies.

We commission the angels to capture every demonic spirit that came with the spirit of fear that came through the back door of this crown.

(What it did was open the door to other spirits.)

We commission the angels to gather up these spirits and take them to be judged—those that infiltrated the mind and the heart, those that brought the lies and instilled the fear.

Lord, we ask in the Courts of Heaven that these inferior spirits be judged on behalf of the sons. We receive Your righteous verdicts on behalf of us and our generations. We ask that these inferior crowns be destroyed. Thank You for the Crown of a New Day—of Your new for us. Thank You for the Superior Crown of the mind of Christ and the Crown of Love. Thank You, Jesus. I ask Father for the healing balm for the wounds. When this inferior Crown of Fear is placed on people's heads, it creates ugly wounds.

Further, we request the destruction of this throne, mantle, and crown by the name and blood of Jesus.

We come out of agreement with the master of this crown. Forgive us where we traded and agreed with it.

Your Honor, we ask for Your righteous verdict or further counsel.

[If further counsel is advised, follow these instructions. Once you have received a righteous verdict, begin the following segment:]

We speak to the Earth on which every one of our generations has stepped, including those related to us by blood, marriage, adoption, or civil and religious covenant.

Earth, we have received a righteous verdict from the Courts of Heaven this day. We bless you to hear the Word of the Lord. We bless you to swallow up the iniquity and the egregious sins of self-deception and wearing these inferior crowns. Swallow up every word and deed that was done upon you. Swallow the innocent bloodshed, sexual sins, moving of the boundary stones, worship of ourselves, idol worship, occultic worship, theft—every sin under the sun that Jesus died for. We charge you to swallow it up and bless you to your original design. We bless you to see the governing sons and to begin blessing us. Begin pouring out your riches of abundance of truth and life.

We request the blood of Jesus to cover every place this was done upon you or in you. We speak to the frequencies of the wind to blow away the evil, to the water to drown it, and to the fire to burn it. We speak to you to return to your original design as the Lord had created you. The Earth is the Lord's, and its fullness belongs to the Lord.

We speak peace. We thank the Just Judge. We thank you, Jesus, the author and the finisher of our faith, for the

Crowns of Righteousness and the Crown of Love that trump this inferior crown.

As governing sons, we pick up these Superior Crowns, place them upon our heads, and ask You to help us rule. We commission the angels to render these righteous verdicts in the spirit and the natural. We commission the angels to put this on record.

Thank you, Just Judge, for honoring us and trusting us with the responsibility of wearing these Crowns of Love and Crowns of Righteousness. Thank you for helping us occupy the territory you assigned us. We don't take this lightly, and we ask for supernatural assistance and help daily to govern as well as Your sons in the name of Jesus.

As sons, we call in the treasure that has been lost from the north, the south, the east, and the west in every age, realm, dimension, and time to fill the capacity of this section.

We ask that all of this be done in time and out of time, and in every age, realm, and dimension, and that all of the spiritual debris, residue, and essences that were left behind by this inferior crown and the spirits that came with it be destroyed utterly. We thank You, Father, for what You did, Jesus, for giving us authority and dominion here.

———— ∞ ————

Chapter 5
The False Crown of Magic

Here are the top twelve characteristics of the false Crown of Magic that you need to recognize and guard against:

1. It is Unusually Beautiful and Alluring. This crown is specifically designed to be enchanting—with stunning purple stones and an elegant, dark, larger design. Its beauty is intentionally captivating, making it one of the most visually appealing traps the enemy sets.

2. It Features Built-In Surveillance Technology. Here's something truly sinister: the crown has a larger stone that acts as an "eye," allowing the enemy to monitor everything the wearer does. It's like having a spiritual spy camera embedded right in your crown! One of the reasons for this surveillance system is that Satan doesn't trust the wearers and wants to keep tabs on what they are doing.

3. It Appears Good but Contains Contaminated Darkness. The crown looks beneficial on the surface, but its "good" is thoroughly contaminated by darkness and falsehood. It is goodness mixed with poison, making it especially deceptive.

4. It is Tantalizing and Uniquely Deceptive. What makes this crown stand out is how tantalizing it is—it creates an almost irresistible pull. The deception comes packaged with witchcraft, making it uniquely dangerous among false crowns.

5. It Promotes the "Good Witch" Lie. This crown pushes the cultural deception that "good witchcraft" can be distinguished from "evil witchcraft." Scripture permits no such distinction—**all** witchcraft is forbidden.

6. It is Worn by Satan's Brides. This crown is specifically associated with those who have entered into spiritual marriage with Satan. It's a crown of unholy union and covenant with darkness.

7. It is Filled with Lust for Power. The crown does not provide true authority—only an insatiable lust for power that never satisfies. It creates an addictive craving for control and influence.

8. It Suspends Wearers in False Elevation. Those who wear it are suspended in a realm of darkness that appears to them as light. They feel elevated and empowered, but the elevation is entirely illusory.

9. It is the Most Dishonoring of All Crowns. This crown brings profound dishonor because it reflects dishonor toward the Lord. Though shame may not appear immediately, its wearers eventually become deeply embedded in shame.

10. It Contains Truth Mixed with Lies. Perhaps most dangerously, this crown has elements of truth that pull people in. But when lies are embedded in truth, the entire thing becomes a lie. It's truth contaminated and weaponized. It works very subtly to accomplish this.

11. It Comes with Insatiable Spiritual Appetite. The spirit of whoring accompanies this crown, creating an insatiable appetite that can never be satisfied. It's handcrafted in the depths of hell with endless craving built into its very design.

12. It is Generationally Transmitted with Attached Spirits. This crown often comes through generational assignments where there has been witchcraft in the bloodline. It attaches lingering human spirits to the generational line, and these spirits will fight to keep the crown because it has empowered them. This witchcraft can manifest as "charismatic witchcraft," where it is disguised as operating within churches and as the manipulation of people and situations.

Summary

The encouraging truth is that light always dispels darkness! When you recognize these characteristics and choose repentance, these crowns can be removed from your generational line. The angels can be commissioned to *blight*—(to completely destroy) these crowns from your bloodline. Though there may be a fight from the spirits who don't want to give up their power, they will be removed when you stand in the authority of Jesus!

Remember: no matter how beautiful, powerful, or "good" witchcraft appears, it's all contaminated. Choose the authentic power and beauty that comes from the Kingdom of Heaven instead!

Structures of the False Crown of Magic

The Beautiful Deception: Understanding the False Crown of Magic

And no wonder, for Satan himself masquerades as an angel of light. (2 Corinthians 11:14, NIV)

The enemy's most sophisticated trap often comes disguised as beauty itself. The Crown of Magic is among the most deceptive of all false crowns—not because it appears dark, but because it presents itself as stunning, beneficial, and spiritually enlightening.

Understanding how this crown functions is not meant to create fear or suspicion. Rather, it equips believers with discernment, enabling them to recognize counterfeits when the Lord desires to bring His people into genuine spiritual authority.

Why This Crown Is Uniquely Dangerous

The Crown of Magic operates through refined deception rather than obvious evil. It attracts people through beauty, promises power through seemingly positive means, and even incorporates elements of truth to make its lies more believable. This makes it particularly dangerous because it can deceive even those who consider themselves spiritually mature.

The Twelve Deceptive Structures

1. The Beauty Trap: Aesthetic Magnetism

This crown is intentionally designed to be visually stunning, featuring elegant purple stones and dark, sophisticated design elements. Its beauty is calculated to override discernment by appealing to the senses rather than the spirit. True discernment looks beyond appearance and evaluates source and fruit. The danger lies in assuming that something beautiful must be good.

2. The Surveillance System: Built-In Monitoring

Perhaps most disturbing is this crown's embedded "surveillance technology," a larger stone that functions as an “eye” allowing constant monitoring of the wearer's activities. This reveals something crucial about the enemy's kingdom: even Satan doesn't trust those who serve him.

Any spiritual authority that requires secrecy, hidden channels, or unaccountable monitoring is inherently suspect.

3. The Contaminated Good: Poisoned Truth

Although the crown appears positive, its “good” is thoroughly corrupted. Truth mixed with error becomes deception. It's like offering pure-looking water that's been laced with poison—the contamination makes the entire substance deadly.

This teaches us that spiritual truth mixed with error becomes error. We must test everything against Scripture, not just accept what seems partially right.

4. The Irresistible Pull: Enchantment-Based Appeal

The crown exerts an almost magnetic pull through enchantment and witchcraft. This supernatural magnetism bypasses rational thought and spiritual discernment, drawing people in through spiritual manipulation rather than genuine conviction.

True spiritual calling never bypasses our will or reasoning capacity—God appeals to our hearts and minds, not our vulnerabilities.

5. The Cultural Lie: "Good" Witchcraft Deception

This crown promotes the myth that "good" witchcraft exists. Scripture recognizes no such category; all witchcraft involves spiritual authorities outside the Lord's Kingdom, regardless of motives or appearance.

6. The Unholy Union: Spiritual Marriage with Darkness

This crown represents a spiritual marriage covenant with Satan. It's not just about practicing magic—it's about entering an actual spiritual union with the enemy.

This reminds us that spiritual practices aren't neutral activities; they involve real spiritual relationships and covenants that have lasting consequences.

7. The Power Addiction: Insatiable Authority Craving

The crown does not offer real authority. It fuels a craving for power that never satisfies, producing dependency and compulsion.

In contrast, authentic spiritual authority comes through service and submission to God, not through acquiring supernatural abilities or influence over others.

8. The False Elevation: Suspended Illusion

Wearers experience a counterfeit realm where darkness appears as light. They feel elevated and powerful while being deceived about their true spiritual condition.

This inversion of reality is characteristic of all false spiritual systems—they make people feel enlightened while leading them deeper into deception.

9. The Ultimate Dishonor: Progressive Shame

This crown brings profound dishonor because it springs from dishonoring the Lord. The shame may not be immediately apparent, but it becomes embedded over time.

This progressive shame reveals that participating in occult practices—no matter how beautiful or beneficial they seem—ultimately leads to spiritual degradation.

10. The Weaponized Truth: Strategic Contamination

This crown incorporates genuine spiritual truths to make its deceptions more believable. When truth is mixed with lies, the entire message becomes corrupt and dangerous.

This is why we need a thorough biblical grounding—not just to recognize obvious lies, but to discern when truth is being used to package deception.

11. The Spiritual Addiction: Insatiable Appetite

The spirit of whoring accompanies the crown, generating an endless spiritual appetite. It's designed to create spiritual addiction and dependency.

This contrasts sharply with a genuine relationship with God, which brings satisfaction, peace, and contentment rather than endless craving.

12. Generational Transmission: Bloodline Bondage

This crown often passes through family lines where witchcraft has been practiced, with attached spirits that fight to maintain their influence. It can even manifest as "charismatic witchcraft" within churches through manipulation disguised as spiritual gifts.

This highlights the importance of dealing with generational spiritual influences and ensuring that spiritual manifestations in church settings are genuinely from God.

Recognizing the Warning Signs

How can we identify this crown's influence?

- **An emphasis on supernatural power** rather than character and service.
- **The presence of secrecy or exclusive spiritual practices** not grounded in Scripture.
- **Spiritual experiences that create addiction** instead of satisfaction.

- **Teaching that contradicts biblical principles** concerning occult practices.
- **Leaders who operate without accountability** or transparency.
- **Spiritual practices that foster dependency** on a leader or system.
- **Beautiful or impressive manifestations** that do not produce the fruit of the Spirit.

Biblical Guidelines for Discernment

Scripture provides clear guidance for evaluating spiritual practices and manifestations:

Test the Spirits (1 John 4:1-3)

Every spiritual manifestation should confess that Jesus Christ has come in the flesh. Anything that doesn't acknowledge Christ's lordship is suspect.

Examine the Fruit (Matthew 7:16-20)

Genuine spiritual authority produces love, joy, peace, patience, kindness, goodness, faithfulness, gentleness, and self-control—not addiction, secrecy, or manipulation.

Seek Accountability (Hebrews 13:17)

True spiritual authority operates within biblical accountability structures, not in isolation or secrecy.

Ground Everything in Scripture (2 Timothy 3:16-17)

Any spiritual practice or teaching should be clearly supported by biblical truth, not just spiritual experience or tradition.

The Path to Authentic Spiritual Authority

God desires to give His people genuine spiritual authority, but it comes through:

Relationship, Not Technique

True spiritual power flows from an intimate relationship with God through Christ, not from learning spiritual techniques or acquiring supernatural abilities.

Service, Not Domination

Biblical spiritual authority expresses itself through humble service to others, not through control or manipulation.

Transparency, Not Secrecy

Genuine spiritual leadership operates in the light, with accountability and transparency, not in hidden or exclusive practices.

Character, Not Just Power

God's priority is developing Christ-like character in us, with spiritual gifts and authority flowing from that foundation.

Breaking Free from Deception

If you recognize any of these influences in your life or spiritual community:

1. **Repent specifically** for any involvement with occult practices—no matter how they were presented.
2. **Renounce any spiritual covenants** or commitments made outside of biblical faith.
3. **Seek deliverance** from any spiritual bondages through biblical prayer ministry.
4. **Ground yourself thoroughly** in Scripture and biblically sound teaching.
5. **Find accountability** with mature believers who can help you discern truth from error.
6. **Focus on relationship** with God rather than pursuing spiritual experiences or power.

A Word of Hope and Caution

The existence of sophisticated spiritual counterfeits shouldn't make us afraid of genuine spiritual gifts and authority that God wants to give His people. Instead, it should cause us to walk carefully, ensuring that what we receive is truly from Him.

Remember that God's gifts are given freely through a relationship with Jesus Christ, not earned through spiritual techniques or practices. His authority comes with peace, not addiction. His truth brings freedom, not bondage. His beauty is pure, not contaminated with darkness.

The Crown of Magic may be beautiful and alluring, but it's no match for the genuine Crown of Life that Christ offers to those who love Him and walk in His truth.

> *But when he, the Spirit of truth, comes, he will guide you into all the truth. (John 16:13, NIV)*

True spiritual discernment comes not from suspicion of everything supernatural, but from knowing God well enough to recognize His genuine work and distinguish it from counterfeits.

Prayer for Removal of the False Crown of Magic

Father, we ask to step into Your Court of Mercy, through Jesus, on behalf of the generations. We ask that the accuser of the brethren be brought in, as well as our generational line, from both sides of the family, and those with us by blood, marriage, adoption, civil or religious covenant—from Your hand in the Garden and forward to Your hand in the future. Your Honor, we agree with the adversary that we were deceived by magic and everything it encompasses.

We repent for magic, for the use of it, for the places in the generations that yielded to it, utilized it, for those who took it up, who felt empowered by it, who were deceived because of it, and for those who elevated themselves in believing the lie.

We repent for those in the generations who practiced magic but also deceived others with bits of truth to pull them into the lie. We repent on their behalf.

We repent on behalf of everyone who believed the lie, succumbed to it, and then projected it and perpetuated it through the generational line.

We repent for agreeing with the spirit of whoring, for trading with it, for seducing because of it, and for allowing it.

We repent for the garments they wore. We ask that they be removed and destroyed now.

We repent, Sir, all the way back to Your hand in the Garden and all the way forward as far as it needs to go. Lord, we repent for taking this inferior crown and for the use of this crown, where they saw it as useful, even though it was a lie.

We repent for the place we put this inferior crown on other people's heads and on our own.

On behalf of the lingering human spirits who are or who are not part of our bloodline, as well as our generations who are now assigned to the bloodline because of taking up these inferior crowns, we repent on their behalf. We repent for every sin under the sun, which is egregious in nature. These sins dishonored and brought dishonor to the Lord because the people took up and wore these inferior crowns.

We commission the angels to go through the timelines, ages, and dimensions for every person who wore this inferior crown, and we commission you to take it off their heads as we stand before the Lord in repentance for them. We forgive, bless, and release them.

We ask the angels to open the silver channel, take the demonic guard and the bosses who were assigned to these lingering human spirits to Jesus's feet for judgment. To every lingering human spirit in the generational line, you will go and see Jesus today. You are not staying.

We forgive you, bless you, and release you for what you were doing in and through the bloodline. You are removed this day by the hand of God because of repentance, which we are allowed to do. He forgave us, and we forgive you.

When you see Jesus, we suggest you ask Him for mercy. Angels, we commission you to destroy every inferior Crown of Witchcraft in the name of Jesus.

We ask for a Crown of Truth to be given to our generational line—the utter and distinct truth, the

Superior Crown that causes all other inferior crowns to be dismantled and destroyed, as their knee must bow, in the name of Jesus.

We ask that the thrones and mantles be found, dismantled, and destroyed in every place throughout the generational line.

Where our generations set this up as a type of altar, we ask that it be destroyed, and that every attendant of every altar be captured and dealt with according to the will of the Father, and that the idol of witchcraft, as well as this Crown of Magic, be judged in the courts today.

We commission the angels to take every spirit or entity who has been assigned or associated with this throne, inferior crown, mantle, and scepter to be taken to court for judgment. We commission the angels to destroy the thrones forever, and that the altar of the Lord be established in their place, in and through the bloodline. We request that angels be assigned there to worship and that the Crown of Truth be established as it sits upon the altar of the Lord.

We request that every false scepter that came with this inferior crown and this throne, which was a wand, also be taken from the generational bloodline and be utterly destroyed, annulled, and removed. We ask that its frequency be dismantled and destroyed in the name of Jesus.

We request that the realm of the inferior hovering crown, the realm from which it came, be closed and that there be a closed, sealed door in and upon the line of the generations forevermore, with no ability to reopen.

We request that the center stone of this inferior crown, which is the eye, be utterly crushed, annulled, canceled, destroyed, and blinded forever in, through, and upon the generational line.

We ask for the amendment of 'As if it Never Were.'

We ask for our righteous verdicts or further counsel.

> [If further counsel is advised, follow these instructions. Once you have received a righteous verdict, begin the following segment:]

We speak to the earth, water, air, and fire. We have received a righteous verdict, and since the world and the fullness of it belong to the Lord, we charge you to swallow up, drown, blow away, and burn all evil words, deeds, lies, witchcraft, innocent bloodshed, sexual sins, occultic cauldrons, evil rooms, evil technologies, spells, hexes, vexes, incantations, voodoo, dark art, manipulation, monitoring, astral projections, evil projections, counterfeit intelligence, and all other darkness or evil done upon the Earth, through the air, to the water and using fire.

We bless you to the fullness of your original design and charge you to bless us as the Lord walks through time, restoring you and it to their fullness. We do this in the name and blood of Jesus and as governing sons.

As sons, we call in the treasure that has been lost from the north, the south, the east, and the west in every age, realm, dimension, and time to fill the capacity of this section.

We ask that all of this be done in time and out of time, and in every age, realm, and dimension, and that all the spiritual debris, residue, and essences left behind by this inferior crown and the spirits that came with it be destroyed utterly. We thank You, Father, for what You did, Jesus, for giving us authority and dominion here.

Stephanie then saw the angel remove the center stone from its mounting and crush it. That's why there is a throne associated with this crown; it is a seat of its power.

The thing about the enemy is that *he doesn't trust anyone,* so embedded in this crown was the eye for him to see what they do for him. It's like back-and-forth messaging. Because he doesn't trust anyone, he sets up a monitoring system in each crown. It is wicked technology.

———— ∞ ————

Chapter 6
The False Crown of Secrets

Let's progress through learning about these false crowns and their structures. The top 12 characteristics of the false Crown of Secrets that you need to recognize and guard against:

1. It Operates Quietly and with Stealth. This crown is unlike any other because it operates in complete stealth-mode. It doesn't announce itself or make obvious moves—it works silently and secretly, making it incredibly dangerous because you might not even realize you're wearing it.

2. It Silences the Sons. One of its primary missions is to silence God's sons and daughters. It knows that when the sons speak up, pray, and intercede, it loses power, so it works overtime to keep you quiet and ineffective. To do this, it will link up with fear to intimidate you.

3. It has a Bloodthirsty, Violent Nature. This crown has a violent, bloodthirsty character that walks together with the spirit of death. It's not just about keeping secrets—it's about destruction and spiritual murder. It may seem polite on the outside, but be aware that it is not the only side of this crown.

4. It Pierces Spiritual Frequencies. The crown specifically targets and disrupts spiritual frequencies, particularly the sounds of intercession. It seeks to pierce through and destroy the spiritual communication between Heaven and Earth. It likes to bring disturbance.

5. It Has Inner Workings of Harlotry, Divination, and Mockery. The crown operates through three specific mechanisms: harlotry (spiritual adultery), divination (false spiritual revelation), and mockery (making fun of what's holy and true). Again, some of the other crowns cooperate with this crown to bring those inner workings to pass.

6. It Works in Partnership with Antichrist. This crown doesn't work alone; it specifically cooperates with the false Crown of Antichrist. It's part of a larger system designed to oppose Christ and His Kingdom.

7. It Has a Hidden, Cloaked Appearance. The dragon's head, wearing this crown, has a cloak around it to keep it hidden. It's deliberately designed to be concealed and undetectable, which makes it particularly insidious.

8. It is Connected to Freemasonry and Secret Organizations. This crown is described as "the seat of Freemasonry" with its own throne. It's directly linked to secret societies and their hierarchical degree systems that create fantasy worlds with elaborate titles.

9. It Defiles the Imagination. The crown specifically targets and corrupts your imagination, creating fantasies that cooperate with spiritual harlotry. It pollutes your creative and visionary capacities with deceptive imagery.

10. Its Mouth is Full of Corruption and Falsehood. This crown speaks of corruption, indignity, and lies. Everything that comes from it is designed to shame, degrade, and deceive rather than build up and encourage.

11. It Seeks to Shame and Silence Through Secrets. The crown uses secrets as weapons to create shame and keep people silent. It knows that hidden things fester and grow in darkness, so it encourages secrecy as a control mechanism.

12. It Contains the Spirit of Regret. This crown carries regret within it—not the healthy conviction that leads to repentance, but the destructive regret that keeps you trapped in shame and prevents you from moving forward in freedom.

Summary

The encouraging truth is that every secret will be revealed, and the Lord is the one who uncovers what needs to be brought to light. The antidote to this crown is transparency, confession, and walking in the fear of the Lord. When you confess your trespasses to one another and pray for each other, healing comes, and this crown loses its power.

Remember: secrets belong to the Lord, but what He reveals belongs to you and your children forever. Choose transparency over secrecy, truth over deception, and the light of God's kingdom over the darkness of hidden things. You have the authority to crush this serpent under your feet and govern well as a son or daughter of the King! If you are prone to holding secrets, the discerning people around you may wonder (1) What are you hiding? and (2) Why are you keeping it hidden?

The Crown You Can't See: Unmasking the False Crown of Secrets

> *But everything exposed by the light becomes visible—and everything that is illuminated becomes a light. (Ephesians 5:13, NIV)*

I want to talk to you today about one of the enemy's most dangerous weapons—and it's one you might never see coming. While other false crowns announce themselves with obvious darkness or dramatic manifestations, the false Crown of Secrets operates like a master spy, working in complete stealth to destroy your spiritual effectiveness without you even knowing it's there.

This crown is particularly sinister because it thrives in the shadows, using secrecy as both its weapon and its shield. Today, we're going to shine the light of truth on this hidden enemy and examine how it operates so you can recognize and guard against its influence.

Why This Crown Is So Dangerous

Before we dive into the specifics, let me help you understand what makes the Crown of Secrets uniquely threatening. Unlike other spiritual attacks that you can feel or see, this crown operates in complete stealth mode. You might be wearing it right now and not even know it. That's not meant to scare you—it's intended to equip you with the knowledge you need to walk in freedom.

The Twelve Hidden Structures

1. The Invisible Enemy: Stealth Operations

The first thing you need to understand about this crown is that it never announces itself. It works silently, secretly, and without fanfare. Think of it as the spiritual equivalent of a computer virus running in the background, slowly corrupting your system while you're completely unaware.

This stealth operation makes it incredibly dangerous because you might not realize you're under attack until significant damage has been done. The crown bypasses your conscious awareness and goes straight to work undermining your spiritual life.

2. The Silencing Strategy: Shutting Down God's Voice

Here's something crucial to understand: this crown has a primary mission to silence God's sons and daughters. Why? Because the enemy knows that when believers speak up, pray boldly, and intercede effectively, his kingdom loses power.

The crown works overtime to keep you quiet and spiritually ineffective. It often partners with the spirit of fear to intimidate you into silence. Have you ever felt like you should speak up in a situation but found yourself mysteriously tongue-tied? This crown might be at work.

3. The Hidden Violence: Bloodthirsty Nature Beneath Politeness

Don't let this crown's quiet operation fool you—beneath its polite exterior lies a violent, bloodthirsty character that partners directly with the spirit of death.

It's not just about keeping secrets; it's about spiritual destruction and murder.

This dual nature makes it particularly deceptive. It presents itself as harmless, maybe even helpful ("Just keep this between us..."), but its true intention is your spiritual demise.

4. The Communication Jammer: Disrupting Heaven's Frequencies

One of this crown's most devastating attacks targets spiritual frequencies—particularly the sounds of intercession and prayer. Think of it as a spiritual jamming device that disrupts communication between Heaven and Earth.

When you find it difficult to pray, when worship feels flat, or when you sense interference during times of intercession, this crown might be creating that spiritual static. It loves to disrupt peaceful spiritual environments.

5. The Triple Threat: Harlotry, Divination, and Mockery

This crown operates through three specific corrupt mechanisms:

- **Spiritual Harlotry** – leading you into unfaithfulness to God through seemingly innocent compromises.

- **Divination** – offering false spiritual revelation that seems enlightening but leads away from truth.
- **Mockery** – encouraging you to make light of holy things or dismiss spiritual matters.

These three work together, often cooperating with other false crowns to maximize their destructive impact.

6. The Dark Alliance: Partnership with Antichrist

This crown doesn't work alone—it's part of a larger system that cooperates specifically with the false Crown of Antichrist. Together, they form a strategic alliance designed to oppose Christ and His Kingdom.

Understanding this partnership helps us realize we're not just dealing with isolated spiritual issues, but with coordinated attacks against God's purposes in our lives.

7. The Perfect Disguise: Cloaked and Hidden

In the spiritual realm, this crown appears with a cloak around it, deliberately designed to remain concealed and undetectable. This intentional invisibility makes it particularly insidious—you can't fight what you can't see.

But here's the good news: once you know what to look for, the Holy Spirit will help you recognize its influence and break its power.

8. The Secret Society Connection: Freemasonry's Throne

This crown is directly connected to secret societies, particularly Freemasonry, and operates as their spiritual headquarters. It thrives on hierarchical degree systems, elaborate titles, and fantasy worlds that promise knowledge and power through secrecy.

If there's been involvement with secret organizations in your family line, this crown may have gained access through that spiritual door.

9. The Imagination Polluter: Corrupting Creative Capacity

One of this crown's most subtle attacks targets your imagination and creative capacity. It does not destroy them—it corrupts them. It stirs fantasies that cooperate with spiritual unfaithfulness and introduces deceptive imagery that leads you away from truth.

If your thought life becomes polluted or your creative expressions begin drifting toward compromise, this crown may be defiling your imagination.

10. The Poison Tongue: Speaking Corruption

Everything that comes from this crown is designed to shame, degrade, and deceive rather than build up and encourage. Its mouth is full of corruption, indignity, and lies.

Pay attention to the internal voices in your head or the "suggestions" that come during quiet moments. Are they building you up in faith, or are they subtly tearing down your confidence in God's love and purposes?

11. The Shame Game: Weaponizing Secrets

This crown's favorite weapon is using secrets to create shame and keep people silent. It understands a fundamental truth: hidden things fester and grow in darkness. The crown encourages secrecy as a control mechanism, knowing that what remains in darkness gains power over us.

The antidote to this weapon is simple but powerful: bringing things into the light.

> *Confess your sins to one another, and pray for one another so that you may be healed. (James 5:16, NASB)*

12. The Regret Trap: Destructive Rather than Redemptive

Finally, this crown carries a spirit of regret—but not the redemptive, God-given conviction that leads to repentance. This is destructive regret that traps you in shame and keeps you from moving forward.

Godly sorrow leads to repentance *without regret* (2 Corinthians 7:10), but this crown produces the kind of regret that paralyzes you in past mistakes instead of propelling you toward God's grace.

Now that we've exposed this crown's tactics, let's talk about how to walk in freedom.

1. Bring Everything into the Light

The crown's power lies in secrecy and darkness. Start exposing hidden things to the light of God's truth and trusted spiritual mentors.

2. Break the Silence

Begin using your voice again—in prayer, in worship, in speaking truth. The enemy worked hard to silence you because your voice has power.

3. Cleanse Your Imagination

Ask the Holy Spirit to purify your thought life and creative capacities. Fill your mind with whatever is true, honorable, just, pure, lovely, and commendable (Philippians 4:8).

4. Remove Secret Society Ties

If there's been involvement with secret organizations in your family line, specifically remove legally those ties and ask for cleansing from generational influences. Utilize my book, *Overcoming the False Verdicts of Freemasonry.*[4]

5. Embrace Healthy Community

Move away from relationships built on secrecy and toward a transparent, godly community where you can be known, healed, and strengthened.

The Power of Exposure

Here's what you must remember: *This crown loses its power the moment it is exposed.* Its entire operation depends on remaining hidden, so the simple act of recognizing its presence begins to break its influence.

You don't have to live under the oppression of secrets, shame, or silence. God has called you to be a voice in this generation, and no crown of darkness can permanently silence what He has destined to speak.

The enemy may operate in stealth, but our God operates in truth, light, and transparency. His truth has the power to set you completely free from every hidden bondage and every secret chain.

---

4. *Overcoming the False Verdicts of Freemasonry: Fourth Edition* by Dr. Ron M. Horner. LifeSpring Publishing, 2025.

As we close this portion, take heart: if you've recognized any of these patterns in your life, don't despair—rejoice! Recognition is the first step toward freedom. The very fact that you can now see these tactics means the light is already beginning to shine in the darkness.

Remember, you serve a God who *"reveals deep and hidden things; he knows what lies in darkness, and light dwells with him"* (Daniel 2:22, NIV). Nothing is hidden from His sight, and nothing is too secret for His power to expose and heal.

Take time today to ask the Holy Spirit to reveal any areas where this crown might be operating. Be willing to bring hidden things into the light. Choose to use your voice for His glory. And watch as the power of secrets, shame, and silence breaks off your life for good.

You were created to walk in the light, speak with authority, and live in complete freedom. Don't let the enemy's stealth tactics convince you otherwise.

Are you ready to step out of the shadows and into the light? The journey to freedom begins with a single step—and today can be that day.

Prayer for Removal of the False Crown of Secrets

Father, we ask for access to Your Court of Mercy today. I repent on behalf of myself and my generations, who kept secrets and willingly took this crown. We reveled in harlotry, took on shame, co-labored with deception, allowed it to mock, and caused the silencing of Your voice. As governing sons, forgive us and our generations for the secrets we held, for having secrets about others, and for using those secrets against them.

We repent for not removing this crown from our own heads, for not confessing our sins one to another so that we could be healed, and for not confessing these things to You. We harbored them in our hearts and acted as though You didn't know. We repent where we behaved as though You could not see, where we kept secrets, and even smiled and reveled in them.

Forgive us and our generations, and forgive us where we took the throne and the seat of Freemasonry within our generations and did not present the throne and the crown to You.

Forgive us and our generations, and forgive us where we took the throne and the seat of Freemasonry within our generational line and did not present the throne and the crown to You. We take it now, and we crush it—this inferior crown under our feet—crushing the head of the snake, the head of this dragon. We present the throne to

You and request that the angels utterly destroy it, and that the altar and the idols of secrecy be judged in Your court this day as we repent on behalf of the generations who did not truly know what they were doing. We ask that every demonic spirit used through this throne and crown be fully captured. Forgive us where Your voice through us was silenced.

Because of this, we ask that angels crush shame and regret. We ask for the amendment of "As if it Never Were," and that as Your blood pours through our generations, the angels would remove every Crown of Secrets in the bloodline and destroy it.

Forgive us when we uncovered others and brought them shame because of the secret we knew.. We accept Father the scripture that everything that is done in secret is brought to light—Your light. We ask this in the name of Jesus.

We thank You, Father; we thank You, Jesus; and we thank You, for your transparency as we learn that transparency is godly—no secrets.

We repent for any and all cooperation with Baal in any form at any time. We turn our back to the altar of Baal and ask angels to destroy every altar of Baal. We ask for a divorce from Baal, Lucifer, the red dragon, the Book of Magic, and any ungodly attraction. We ask that all debris associated with this cooperation with Baal be removed and destroyed on our behalf. We remove the regalia associated with this ungodly marriage covenant and request to be clothed in robes of righteousness.

We request that the head of this snake be cut off from the other heads and from this dragon.

We ask for Your righteous verdict or further counsel.

> [If further counsel is advised, follow these instructions. Once you have received a righteous verdict, begin the following segment:]

We speak to the Earth on which every one of our generations has stepped, including those related to us by blood, marriage, adoption, or civil and religious covenant.

Earth, we have received a righteous verdict from the Courts of Heaven this day. We bless you to hear the word of the Lord. We bless you to swallow up the iniquity and the egregious sins of self-deception and wearing these inferior crowns. Swallow up every word and deed that was done upon you. Swallow the innocent bloodshed, sexual sins, moving of the boundary stones, worship of ourselves, idol worship, occultic worship, theft—every sin under the sun that Jesus died for. We charge you to swallow it up and bless you to your original design. We bless you to see the governing sons and to begin blessing us. Begin pouring out your riches of abundance, truth, and life.

We request the blood of Jesus to cover every place this was done upon you or in you. We speak to the frequencies of the wind to blow away the evil, to the water to drown it, and to the fire to burn it. We speak to you to return to your original design as the Lord had created you. The Earth is the Lord's, and its fullness belongs to the Lord.

We speak peace. We thank the Just Judge. We thank You, Jesus, the author and the finisher of our faith, for the Crowns of Righteousness and the Crown of Love that trump this inferior crown.

As governing sons, we pick up these Superior Crowns, place them upon our heads, and ask You to help us rule. We commission the angels to render these righteous verdicts in the spirit and the natural. We commission the angels to put this on record.

Thank You, Just Judge, for honoring us and trusting us with the responsibility of wearing these Crowns of Love and Righteousness. Thank You for helping us occupy the territory You assigned us. We don't take this lightly and ask for supernatural assistance and help daily to govern well as Your sons, in the name of Jesus.

As sons, we call in the treasure that has been lost from the north, the south, the east, and the west in every age, realm, dimension, and time to fill the capacity of this section.

We ask that all of this be done in time and out of time, and in every age, realm, and dimension, and that all of the spiritual debris, residue, and essences that were left behind by this inferior crown and the spirits that came with it be destroyed utterly. We thank You, Father, for what You did, Jesus, for giving us authority and dominion here.

Remembert, these secrets are nothing but lies. There's no truth in them. If this head has a secret, he is not revealing it.

However, Mark 4:22 says:

> *For there* ***is nothing that is hidden that won't be disclosed,*** *and* ***there is no secret that won't be brought out into the light!*** *(TPT, Emphasis mine)*

We knew we had one more crown to learn about, but a summary of the characteristics of this crown is in order.

Instructions to the Sons:

- Remove and utterly destroy this crown from your heads. It is unbecoming of a son.
- Repent for any involvement with this crown at any time, in any fashion, in any place.
- You are to govern this crown, then remove it, then destroy it.
- Crush this serpent under your feet.

—— ∞ ——

Chapter 7

The False Crown of Antichrist

Here are the top 12 characteristics of the false Crown of Antichrist that you need to recognize and guard against:

1. It is Full of Pomp and Circumstance with an Elite Attitude. This crown creates an atmosphere of grandiose ceremony and self-importance. Those who wear it develop a "better than you" attitude, with deep-seated elitism that looks down on others as inferior.

2. It Contains an Air of Superiority Like the Sadducees. Just like the religious leaders in Jesus' time, this crown creates a superiority complex that makes people think they're spiritually above others. It's the same arrogant spirit that Jesus confronted in the New Testament.

3. It Creates Indoctrinated Followers. Those who wear this crown become completely indoctrinated into false belief systems. They're not just influenced, they're thoroughly programmed and can't see beyond the deception they've embraced.

4. It Works in Network with Other False Crowns. This crown is a master collaborator. It specifically works with the Crown of Secrets and Crown of Deceit and can easily place the Crown of Deception on people's heads. It's like a spiritual networking system of evil.

5. It Clings to the Cross but in Defilement. Here's what makes it so deceptive—this crown appears Christian and clings to the cross, but it defiles everything it touches—it uses Christian symbols and language while corrupting their true meaning.

6. It is Superstitious and Fame-Seeking. This crown makes people superstitious, pretentious, and constantly seeking fame and recognition. It's driven by pride, loftiness, arrogance, and a judgmental spirit toward others.

7. It Has Infiltrated the Church. Perhaps most alarming, this crown has successfully penetrated the church itself! It's not just affecting the world—it's corrupting the Body of Christ from within through compromised leadership.

8. It Calls in Delilah, Jezebel, and Ahab Spirits. This crown attracts and empowers some of the most destructive spiritual forces mentioned in Scripture—spirits of seduction, control, manipulation, and weak leadership that destroy God's people.

9. It Has the Deadliest Bite with Multiple Poisons. While it may appear harmless on the surface, this crown has the deadliest bite of all the false crowns. Its bite contains multiple spiritual poisons that can destroy faith and spiritual life.

10. It Has Led More People Astray Than Any Other Crown. This is the most dangerous crown because it has successfully led more people away from the truth than any other false crown. It's particularly effective at causing spiritual shipwreck.

11. It Operates Through Secret Organizations in the Church. This crown specifically works through Freemasonry and Eastern Star infiltration within churches. Many pastors and spiritual leaders are unknowingly (or knowingly) connected to these secret societies.

12. It Causes People to Leave the Body of Christ Permanently. Those bitten by people wearing this crown often leave the church and never return. We've seen pastors suddenly announce they no longer believe in God—this crown's influence is behind such tragic departures.

Summary

The sobering truth is that this crown's primary goal is **to bring an end to the embodiment of the church!** It creates delusions of grandeur, promotes secrecy, and enslaves people under false spiritual authority.

But here's the encouraging news: you have the authority to deal with this crown! You can remove its mantle, destroy its seat, close its portal, break the chains of enslavement, and cut off the head of this snake from the rest of the dragon system.

Remember, this crown may have an office, a realm, and a spirit behind it, but greater is He who is in you than he who is in the world. You can recognize this crown's characteristics, reject its influence, and help others find freedom from its deadly bite. Choose authentic humility over false superiority, transparency over secrecy, and the true cross over its defiled counterfeit!

Structures of The False Crown of Antichrist

The Enemy's Most Dangerous Weapon: Exposing the False Crown of Antichrist

Watch out for false prophets. They come to you in sheep's clothing, but inwardly they are ferocious wolves. (Matthew 7:15, NIV)

I need to share something urgent with you today. Of all the false crowns we've discussed, there's one that stands above the rest in terms of sheer destructive power—the false Crown of Antichrist. This isn't just another spiritual weapon in the enemy's arsenal; it's his masterpiece of deception, specifically designed to destroy the church from within while masquerading as godly leadership.

What makes this crown so dangerous is that it doesn't attack from the outside, where we might recognize it. Instead, it infiltrates the very heart of the Body of Christ, using Christian language, symbols, and ceremonies to accomplish its devastating work. Today, we're going to pull back the curtain on this ultimate deception so you can recognize it, resist it, and help others find freedom from its deadly influence.

Why This Crown Is the Most Dangerous

Let me be clear: this crown has led more people astray from faith than any other false crown in existence. It's particularly effective because it looks so right on the surface. It clings to the cross, uses biblical language, and operates within church structures. But like a beautiful apple with a rotten core, everything it touches becomes defiled and corrupted.

The sobering truth is that this crown's primary goal is to bring an end to the embodiment of the church itself. But here's what I want you to remember as we dive into its tactics: you have complete authority in Christ to overcome its influence and help others find freedom.

1. The Elite Attitude: Pomp, Circumstance, and Superiority

This crown creates an atmosphere of grandiose ceremony and self-importance that would make a royal court jealous. Those wearing it develop a "better than you" attitude with deep-seated elitism that looks down on others as spiritually inferior.

You'll recognize this in leaders who seem more concerned with titles, ceremonies, and status than with genuinely serving God's people. They create hierarchies that separate the "spiritual elite" from the "common believers."

2. The Sadducee Spirit: Religious Superiority Complex

Just like the religious leaders Jesus confronted, this crown creates the exact same arrogant spirit that thinks it's spiritually above everyone else. It's the Pharisaical attitude that Jesus opposed so strongly in the Gospels.

When you encounter believers who act like they have exclusive access to spiritual truth or who condescend to other Christians, you're likely seeing this crown's influence.

3. The Programming System: Creating Indoctrinated Followers

This crown doesn't just influence people—it completely indoctrinates them into false belief systems. These followers become so thoroughly programmed that they can't see beyond the deception they've embraced, even when presented with clear biblical truth.

The scary part is that these people often seem very sincere and committed. They're not pretending—they genuinely believe the distorted version of Christianity they've been taught.

4. The Master Collaborator: Networking with Other False Crowns

Here's something crucial to understand: this crown is a master collaborator that works specifically with the Crown of Secrets and Crown of Deceit. It can easily place the Crown of Deception on people's heads, creating a spiritual networking system of evil.

This is why false teaching often comes packaged with secrecy, deception, and pride. These crowns work together to create maximum spiritual damage.

5. The Great Defilement: Clinging to the Cross While Corrupting It

Perhaps the most deceptive aspect of this crown is how it clings to Christian symbols and language while defiling everything it touches. It uses the cross, biblical terminology, and Christian traditions, but corrupts their true meaning.

This makes it incredibly hard to detect because it sounds so right and looks so spiritual. The corruption is subtle but devastating.

6. The Fame Game: Superstition and Recognition-Seeking

This crown makes people superstitious, pretentious, and constantly seeking fame and recognition. It's driven by pride, loftiness, arrogance, and a judgmental spirit toward others.

You'll see this in leaders who seem more concerned with building their platform, gaining followers, or receiving recognition than with genuinely shepherding God's people.

7. The Internal Attack: Church Infiltration

Here's what should alarm every believer: this crown has successfully penetrated the church itself. It's not just affecting the world—it's corrupting the Body of Christ from within through compromised leadership.

This isn't about pointing fingers or creating paranoia. It's about recognizing that the enemy's most effective strategy is internal corruption rather than external persecution.

8. The Deadly Alliance: Summoning Destructive Spirits

This crown attracts and empowers some of the most destructive spiritual forces mentioned in Scripture:

Delilah spirits (seduction and betrayal), Jezebel spirits (control and manipulation), and Ahab spirits (weak, compromised leadership).

When you see these patterns in church leadership—seduction, control, manipulation, and weakness—this crown is likely involved.

9. The Deadliest Bite: Multiple Spiritual Poisons

While it may appear harmless on the surface, this crown has the deadliest bite of all false crowns. Its bite contains multiple spiritual poisons that can destroy faith and spiritual life.

The tragedy is that people often don't realize they've been "bitten" until significant spiritual damage has already occurred.

10. The Ultimate Deceiver: Leading More People Astray

This is the most statistically successful crown for destroying faith. It has led more people away from authentic Christianity than any other false crown, and it's particularly effective at causing complete spiritual shipwreck.

The reason it's so successful is that it operates from within trusted spiritual environments, making its deception harder to detect.

11. The Secret Society Connection: Freemasonry and Eastern Star

This crown works explicitly through secret organizations that have infiltrated churches, particularly Freemasonry and Eastern Star. Many pastors and spiritual leaders are connected to these societies, either knowingly or unknowingly.

The combination of Christian appearance with secret society influence creates a particularly toxic spiritual environment that can destroy churches from within.

12. The Final Blow: Permanent Spiritual Departure

Perhaps most tragically, those who are "bitten" by people wearing this crown often leave the church and never return. We've seen pastors suddenly announce they no longer believe in God—this crown's influence is behind such heartbreaking departures.

This crown doesn't just wound people spiritually; it often creates permanent separation from the Body of Christ.

Recognizing the Warning Signs

So how do you recognize this crown's influence? Look for these red flags:

- **Excessive emphasis on hierarchy and titles** rather than servant leadership
- **Secret meetings or exclusive groups** within church leadership

- **Spiritual pride and elitism** that create "us versus them" mentalities.
- **Corruption of biblical symbols** or traditions for personal gain
- **Leadership that seeks fame** more than faithfully serving God's people
- **Manipulation and control** disguised as spiritual authority.
- **Compromise with worldly systems** while maintaining a Christian appearance.

The Path to Victory

Here's the encouraging news I promised: you have complete authority to deal with this crown! In Christ, you can:

- **Remove its mantle** and destroy its seat of power.
- **Close its portal** of influence and break chains of spiritual enslavement.
- **Cut off the head** of this snake from the rest of the dragon system.
- **Expose its deception** and help others find freedom.

Greater is He who is in you than he who is in the world, (1 John 4:4, NASB)

1. Choose Authentic Humility Over False Superiority

Embrace the servant-leadership model Jesus demonstrated rather than hierarchical power structures that elevate some over others.

2. Embrace Transparency Over Secrecy

Be wary of any spiritual leadership that operates in secrecy or creates exclusive inner circles. God's kingdom operates in the light.

3. Follow the True Cross Over Its Defiled Counterfeit

Study Scripture carefully to understand what genuine Christianity looks like versus religious systems that use Christian language but operate by different principles.

4. Test Everything Against Scripture

Don't just accept teaching because it comes from someone in leadership. Be like the Bereans who *"examined the Scriptures every day to see if what Paul said was true"* (Acts 17:11, NIV).

5. Seek Godly Community

Surround yourself with believers who demonstrate genuine humility, transparency, and love for God's Word above personal recognition.

A Word of Hope and Encouragement

I know this might feel overwhelming or even frightening. You might be wondering if you can trust any spiritual leadership, or you might be recognizing some of these patterns in your own church or spiritual community.

Here's what I want you to remember: God is not caught off guard by any of this. He knows precisely where this crown is operating, and He's raising up a generation of believers who can discern truth from deception.

Your job isn't to become suspicious of everyone or to abandon the church. Your assignment is to:

- **Stay close to Jesus** through His Word and prayer.
- **Develop spiritual discernment** through the Holy Spirit.
- **Stand for truth** with love and humility.
- **Help others** recognize and break free from deception.

The Church Will Prevail

Despite this crown's devastating influence, I have absolute confidence in this truth: the gates of hell will not prevail against Christ's church (Matthew 16:18). The enemy may have his counterfeit systems, but God is building His authentic church with people who choose truth over deception, humility over pride, and transparency over secrecy.

You are part of that authentic church. You have been given discernment to recognize these tactics and authority to overcome them. Don't be discouraged by the enemy's counterfeits—be encouraged that God has equipped you to help establish the real thing.

The false Crown of Antichrist may be the enemy's masterpiece of deception, but it's no match for the authentic Crown of Life that Jesus offers to those who love Him. Choose wisely, stand firmly, and help others find the freedom that comes only through a genuine relationship with Christ.

The enemy's greatest deceptions often wear the most convincing disguises. But truth has a way of shining through the darkness, and those who seek it with pure hearts will always find it. Keep seeking, keep discerning, and keep standing for the authentic gospel of Jesus Christ.

Prayer for Removal of the False Crown of Antichrist

Father, we ask to step into the Mercy Court of Heaven to receive Mercy in our time of need. We request the accuser of the brethren be brought in, as well as our entire generations and everyone related to us by blood, marriage, adoption, civil or religious covenant, all the way back to Your hand in the Garden, and all the way forward as far as it needs to go.

Your Honor, we agree with the adversary that we and our generations bowed the knee to this dragon, accepted inferior crowns, and wore them proudly. We repent for the spirit of antichrist we bore and the inferior crown we took upon our heads. We repent for the pomp and circumstance, elitism, "better than you" attitude, superiority complex, indoctrination we took on, as well as the indoctrination of others; we repent for embodying a false religion and for "biting" those we were in stewardship over, releasing the poison. We repent for working with the false Crown of Delusion and the false Crown of Secrets. We repent for all the secrets this inferior crown bore that we agreed with.

We repent for conspiring with the office, realm, and spirit of antichrist, for embodying it, and for participating in exploiting, polluting, and poisoning the church, the Body, and the ecclesia. We repent for contributing to the destruction of ecclesias, people, and churches. We repent for allowing, tolerating, and cooperating with the Delilah, Jezebel, and Ahab spirits. We repent for opening evil portals and for creating evil timelines for ourselves, our generations, and others. We repent for taking on this mantle, sitting on the seat, office, and throne, and ruling unjustly over Your people. We repent for seeking positions of power, and for elevating those who should never have been elevated. We repent for pride, for lusting after power, and for greed.

We repent for falsely clinging to the cross, for defiling and mocking it, for seeking fame, for being pretentious, prideful, lofty, arrogant, and judgmental toward others. We repent for embodying and promoting false religion. Forgive us and our generations for infiltrating the Church with this inferior crown and for elevating others into it. Forgive us for leading others astray.

We request Your blood, Jesus, the amendment of "As If It Never Were," the destruction of the seat, office, and throne, the closing of the portal, and the removal of the garments. Please remove its mantle, destroy the seat, and close the portal. Break the chains from those who have been impacted or who agreed with those who wore this inferior crown across the generations and in our spheres of influence.

Please have these destroyed. We request that the chains attached to us and our generations be cut, severed, destroyed, dismantled, and the ashes of them be brought to Jesus. We request a complete destruction, annulment, cancellation, and overturning of the office of the Crown of Antichrist, in the name of Jesus.

We also request that the angels clean up the spiritual debris, essences, and residues in time, out of time, and in every age, realm, and dimension to infinity. Burn it and give the ashes to Jesus.

We ask for Your righteous verdict or further counsel.

[If further repentance is needed, follow the instructions of the court.]

With our righteous verdict in hand, we speak to the Earth—every place our generations stepped upon, including those related to us by blood, marriage, adoption, civil or religious covenant. Earth, we have received a righteous verdict from the Courts of Heaven this day.

We bless you to hear the word of the Lord. We bless you to swallow up the iniquity and the egregious sins of wearing these inferior crowns. Swallow up every word and deed that was done upon you. Swallow the innocent bloodshed, sexual sins, moving of the boundary stones, worship of ourselves, idol worship, occultic worship, theft—every sin under the sun that Jesus died for.

We charge you to swallow it up, and we bless you to return to your original design. We bless you to recognize the governing sons and begin blessing us. Pour out your riches, abundance, and the truth of life. We request the blood of Jesus to cover every place this was done upon you and within you. To the wind: blow away the evil. To the water: drown it. To the fire: burn it. Return to your original design as the Lord created you. The earth is the Lord's, and the fullness of it belongs to Him.

We speak peace, and we thank You, Jesus. We thank the Just Judge. We thank You, Jesus, the author and the finisher of our faith. We commission the angels to render these righteous verdicts in the spirit and the natural. We commission the angels to put this on record.

Thank You, Just Judge, for honoring us and trusting us with the responsibility of wearing the Crown of Love and Crown of Righteousness. Thank You for helping us occupy the territory You assigned us. We don't take this lightly and ask for supernatural assistance and help daily to govern well as Your sons, in the name of Jesus.

As sons, we call in the treasure that has been lost from the north, the south, the east, and the west in every age, realm, dimension, and time to fill the capacity of this section.

We are grateful to Heaven for revealing the red dragon, its inferior crowns, and its mission. We are grateful that Revelation tells us that this dragon has been pierced by God himself. Thank You for Your kindness in helping us overcome the word of our testimony and the blood of the Lamb.

We ask that all of this be done in time and out of time, in every age, realm, and dimension, and that all spiritual debris, residue, and essences left behind by this inferior crown and the spirits that accompanied it be utterly destroyed. Thank You, Father, for what You did, Jesus, for giving us authority and dominion here.

———— ∞ ————

Chapter 8

The False Crown of Devouring

Listed here are the top 12 characteristics of the false Crown of Devouring that you need to recognize and guard against:

1. It Actively Hunts the Vulnerable. This crown doesn't wait passively—it actively seeks and hunts after sons and daughters, specifically targeting those who are weak or on the edge. It's like a predator that deliberately stalks its prey.

2. It Follows the Stench of Sin. Here's something chilling—this crown can literally smell sin! When there's unrepented sin in your life, it leaves a spiritual stench that this dragon follows like a bloodhound tracking a scent trail.

3. It is In League with Sons of Perdition. This crown works specifically with the sons of perdition—those who have completely given themselves over to darkness, also called Sons of Belial. It's connected to the deepest levels of spiritual rebellion.

4. It is Lethal and Final. Unlike other crowns, which people might recover from, this one is described as lethal. Most people don't return once this crown is placed upon their head—it represents a point of no return spiritually.

5. It Destroys All Sensibility and Reason. This crown makes people lose all common sense and reasonable thinking. When you see someone who has completely "lost their minds" and can't be reasoned with, this crown is likely involved.

6. It Creates Complete Hardness of Heart. Those who wear this crown have the hardest hearts possible. It's not just resistance to God—it's complete spiritual calcification where no tenderness remains.

7. It Goes Beyond Atheism to Active God-Hatred. This isn't just disbelief—it's active, burning hatred of God. It represents a turning away that's far more intense than typical unbelief or skepticism.

8. It Devours Common Sense and God-Connection. The crown specifically seeks to devour people's ability to hear God's voice or see Him. It systematically destroys the common sense and spiritual sensitivities that connect people to divine truth.

9. It Represents Complete Darkness with No Light. Those wearing this crown have absolutely no light in them— only darkness. There's no mixture, no gray area—it's complete spiritual blackness and absence of any divine influence.

10. It is Associated with the Darkest Evil. This crown is worn by those who commit the most heinous acts—like consuming babies, murder, and other unspeakable evils. Think Adolf Hitler and his assistants—that level of darkness.

11. It Works in Tandem with All Other Crowns. This crown doesn't work alone—it collaborates with and amplifies all the other false crowns because its ultimate goal is to devour everything good, true, and godly.

12. It Creates Complete Loss of Conscience. Perhaps most terrifying, this crown removes all conscience. Those who wear it don't just choose evil—they have no internal moral compass left to guide them away from it.

Summary

The sobering truth is that this crown represents the final stage of spiritual rebellion—the point at which someone becomes completely unreachable and unreasonable. But here's the encouraging news: you can protect yourself by keeping sin out of your life, staying close to God, and ensuring the other false crowns are removed first.

Remember, this dragon is roaming about seeking whom he may devour, but you don't have to be his prey! Stay in the love of God, pray in the Holy Spirit, build yourself up in your most holy faith, and hate even the garments defiled by the flesh. The key is not giving this crown a foothold through unrepented sin or agreements with lesser false crowns.

You have the authority to recognize this crown's influence and protect both yourself and others from its devastating effects!

Structures of the False Crown of Devouring

The Ultimate Destroyer: Understanding the False Crown of Devouring

Be alert and of sober mind. Your enemy the devil prowls around like a roaring lion looking for someone to devour. (1 Peter 5:8, NIV)

Today, we need to discuss the most terrifying and final of all false crowns—the Crown of Devouring. This isn't just another spiritual weapon in the enemy's arsenal; it represents the ultimate expression of spiritual destruction and the final stage of spiritual corruption. While other crowns deceive, manipulate, or corrupt, this crown completely devours everything good, true, and godly in a person.

I approach this topic with sober awareness of its reality and confidence in Christ's ultimate victory. While this crown represents the deepest spiritual darkness possible, it's crucial to understand that no one accidentally stumbles into wearing it. There are clear warning signs and pathways that lead to this point, and God's grace provides numerous opportunities for repentance and restoration before reaching this final stage.

Why This Crown Is in a Category by Itself

The Crown of Devouring operates as what can only be described as the "master crown," coordinating with all other false crowns to achieve complete spiritual destruction. It doesn't just influence or corrupt—it completely devours and eliminates every trace of light, conscience, and divine connection.

What makes this crown uniquely terrifying is its finality. Unlike other crowns, where people might recover, this one represents a point of spiritual no return. It's the crown worn by those who have completely given themselves over to darkness and have systematically destroyed every bridge back to the light.

The Ultimate Spiritual Destroyer

This crown operates as the final coordinator of all deceptive systems, with one ultimate goal: to devour everything good, true, and godly in a person. It represents a point of spiritual no return where light, conscience, and divine connection are eliminated.

Understanding this crown isn't about becoming paranoid, but about recognizing the serious consequences of persistent spiritual rebellion and the incredible value of God's grace that keeps us from such darkness.

The Twelve Structures of Complete Destruction

1. The Predator System: Active Spiritual Hunting

This crown doesn't wait for victims—it actively hunts, specifically targeting God's sons and daughters who are vulnerable, weak, or "on the edge" spiritually. It operates through strategic exploitation of vulnerabilities with a deliberate predator-prey dynamic.

This reminds us why spiritual community and accountability are so vital. Isolation and spiritual weakness create vulnerability to attacks that seek our complete destruction.

2. The Sin-Tracking System: Supernatural Detection

Perhaps most sobering is this crown's ability to literally track unrepented sin like a bloodhound following a scent trail. Unconfessed sin creates a spiritual stench that this crown uses to navigate to targets.

This underscores the critical importance of regular confession and repentance—not from legalism, but because undealt-with sin creates vulnerability to spiritual predators.

3. The Dark Alliance: Partnership with Ultimate Rebellion

This crown works specifically with those described as "sons of perdition"—people completely given over to darkness and spiritual rebellion. It forms alliances with the deepest levels of spiritual rebellion, partnering with those considered beyond redemption.

This alliance structure reveals that spiritual rebellion isn't individual—it connects people with increasingly dark spiritual networks and influences.

4. The Finality Framework: Point of No Return

This crown is described as lethal, representing complete spiritual death. Most people don't return once it's placed because it creates an irreversible spiritual condition—the ultimate spiritual terminus.

This finality emphasizes why responding to God's conviction while we can is so crucial. There appears to be a point where persistent rejection of God's grace leads to spiritual conditions from which recovery becomes impossible.

5. The Cognitive Destroyer: Complete Mental Corruption

This crown destroys all common sense and reasonable thinking, creating a complete loss of rational thought processes. People become unable to be reasoned with on any level—they've truly "lost their minds" in the most tragic sense.

When someone reaches this point, normal appeals to reason, conscience, or relationship become ineffective because these faculties have been systematically destroyed.

6. The Heart Killer: Total Spiritual Calcification

This crown creates the most complete hardness of heart possible—not just resistance to God, but complete spiritual calcification, with no tenderness remaining. It's a total emotional and spiritual shutdown with absolute spiritual insensitivity.

This represents a hardness that goes beyond what we typically encounter, in which every capacity for spiritual response has been eliminated.

7. The God-Hater: Beyond Atheism to Active Warfare

This crown goes far beyond disbelief to create burning, active hatred of God. It's not passive rejection but militant opposition and hostility toward everything divine—a warfare stance against God Himself.

This active hatred represents something far more intense than typical unbelief or even angry rejection of faith.

8. The Connection Severer: Divine Communication Destroyer

This crown systematically destroys the ability to hear God's voice, eliminates the capacity to see God working, and devours all spiritual sensitivities. It severs every connection to divine truth and destroys natural God-awareness.

Even non-believers typically retain some capacity to sense God's presence or recognize spiritual truth, but this crown eliminates even that basic spiritual sensitivity.

9. The Light Eliminator: Complete Darkness

Those wearing this crown have absolutely no light left—only darkness, with no mixtures or gray areas. It's complete spiritual blackness with total absence of any divine influence—a complete spiritual void.

This represents darkness so complete that not even the smallest spark of divine light can exist or operate within the person.

10. The Evil Facilitator: Darkest Acts Enablement

This crown is associated with the most heinous acts imaginable—consuming babies, murder, and unspeakable evils. It represents the level of darkness we see in historical figures like Adolf Hitler and enables the most extreme forms of human wickedness.

This connection to ultimate depravity shows what becomes possible when all light and conscience are eliminated from a person.

11. The Master Coordinator: Crown Amplification System

This crown works in tandem with all other false crowns, amplifying their effects and coordinating their destructive work. It serves as the master coordinator of all deceptive crown systems.

This coordination reveals that the enemy's deceptive systems don't work in isolation—they're part of a comprehensive strategy for complete spiritual destruction.

12. The Conscience Killer: Moral Compass Destruction

Perhaps most terrifying, this crown completely removes all conscience. People don't just choose evil—they have no capacity to choose otherwise because their moral faculties have been completely shut down.

This represents the most tragic spiritual condition possible: the complete elimination of the internal moral guidance that God gives every person.

The Critical Warning Signs

While this crown represents a final stage, there are warning signs along the pathway:

- **Persistent, unrepented sin** that creates spiritual vulnerability
- **Increasing isolation** from godly influence and accountability
- **Growing hardness** toward spiritual conviction or truth
- **Progressive association** with darker spiritual influences
- **Increasing cruelty** and lack of empathy toward others
- **Active opposition** to God and His people
- **Loss of the ability** to distinguish right from wrong

The Prevention and Protection

The existence of this crown should motivate us toward:

1. **Immediate Response to Conviction**

Never harden your heart when God speaks. Respond quickly to the Holy Spirit's prompting toward repentance and change.

2. **Regular Spiritual Cleansing**

Maintain regular confession and repentance to avoid creating “scent trails” of undealt-with sin.

3. **Protective Community**

Stay connected to mature believers who can provide accountability, encouragement, and protection through prayer.

4. **Aggressive Pursuit of Light**

Actively seek God's presence, truth, and righteousness rather than passively hoping to avoid darkness.

5. **Intercession for Others**

Pray earnestly for those you see moving in dangerous spiritual directions while they can still respond.

A Message of Hope and Urgency

This information about the Crown of Devouring serves two critical purposes:

First, it should create **profound gratitude** for God's grace that has kept us from such darkness and continues to offer forgiveness and transformation to anyone who will respond.

Second, it should create **holy urgency** to share the gospel and to intercede for those we see moving in dangerous spiritual directions, knowing that there may be a point beyond which recovery becomes impossible.

The existence of this ultimate spiritual destroyer should never create despair about God's power or doubt about His love. Instead, it should deepen our appreciation for His grace and intensify our commitment to walking in His light.

The Greater Reality

While the Crown of Devouring represents ultimate spiritual destruction, we serve the One who is ultimately victorious over all darkness. Even this final crown cannot overcome the power of Christ's death and resurrection for those who call upon His name.

Your responsibility isn't to live in fear of this crown, but to walk confidently in God's light.

Your responsibility isn't to live in fear of this crown, but to walk confidently in God's light, respond quickly to His conviction, and help others find salvation while it's still available.

The enemy may have weapons of ultimate destruction, but our God has the power of ultimate salvation. Choose His light, respond to His love, and help others find the narrow path that leads to life.

Enter through the narrow gate. For wide is the gate and broad is the road that leads to destruction, and many enter through it. But small is the gate and narrow the road that leads to life, and only a few find it. (Matthew 7:13-14, NIV)

The path to destruction may be wide, but the path to life is always available to those who seek it while they can.

The Warning Signs and Pathways

While this crown represents the final stage of spiritual corruption, it doesn't happen overnight. There are clear warning signs and pathways that lead to this point:

Progressive Spiritual Hardening

- **Repeated rejection of conviction**
- **Persistent, unrepented sin** creates spiritual "scent trails."
- **Increasing resistance** to spiritual truth and correction
- **Growing hostility** toward God and His people

Alliance Formation

- **Association with increasingly dark influences**
- **Isolation from godly relationships** and accountability

- **Attraction to occult or rebellious spiritual practices**
- **Progressive compromise** with darker spiritual forces

Moral Erosion

- **Gradual conscience-searing** through repeated wrong choices
- **Justification of increasingly evil behaviors**
- **Loss of the ability to distinguish** right from wrong
- **Growing appetite** for destructive and harmful activities

Protection and Prevention

The good news is that God provides clear warnings and multiple opportunities for repentance before anyone reaches this final stage:

Stay Connected to Light

- **Maintain regular confession and repentance.**
- **Stay in a healthy spiritual community.**
- **Remain accountable** to mature believers.
- **Guard your heart** against bitterness and unforgiveness.

Respond to Conviction

- **Don't harden your heart** when God speaks.
- **Respond quickly** to the Holy Spirit's conviction.
- **Seek help immediately** when struggling with persistent sin.
- **Don't isolate yourself** when facing spiritual battles.

Maintain Spiritual Sensitivity

- **Cultivate regular prayer and worship.**
- **Stay grounded in Scripture.**
- **Surround yourself with godly influences.**
- **Flee from evil** and everything associated with darkness.

Hope for Those Still Reachable

If you recognize some of these warning signs in yourself or someone you care about, remember that as long as there's any conviction, any desire for God, any recognition of right and wrong, there's still hope for complete restoration.

The Crown of Devouring represents the final stage, but until someone reaches that point of complete spiritual death, God's grace is still available, and His power is still sufficient for complete transformation.

A Word of Caution and Comfort

This information isn't meant to create fear or paranoia, but rather to help us understand the serious progression of spiritual rebellion and the importance of responding to God's conviction while we can.

The reality of this crown should motivate us to:

- **Take sin seriously** and deal with it quickly.
- **Maintain tender hearts** toward God and others.
- **Pray earnestly** for those we see moving in dangerous spiritual directions.
- **Share the gospel boldly** while people can still respond.
- **Live in gratitude** for God's grace that keeps us from such darkness.

The light shines in the darkness, and the darkness has not overcome it. (John 1:5, NIV)

No matter how dark the darkness, the light of Jesus is always stronger. Walk in His light, stay connected to His love, and help others find their way to freedom before it's too late.

Prayer for Removal of the False Crown of Devouring

[Repentance for this crown needs to follow repentance for all the other crowns.]

Father, we ask to step into Your Court of Mercy to receive mercy in our time of need. We ask that the accuser of the brethren be brought into this court as well as our generations, those related to us by blood, marriage, civil and religious covenant, all the way back to Your hand in the Garden and all the way forward as far as it needs to go.

Your Honor, this Crown of Devouring cannot be removed until the other crowns are removed. However, we would like to begin the court case process today.

Your Honor, we repent for ourselves and our generations for partnering with, agreeing with, and participating in the darkest of the darkest of sins. We repent that we put ourselves and our generations in danger of being hunted because of these sins. We repent for our weaknesses in not seeking after God. We repent for our generations' sins, which created a stench the enemy could sniff out.

We repent for living on the edge, allowing this dragon to hunt us and those in our generations. We repent for being in league with the sons of perdition—the ones that have given themselves over to darkness. We repent for losing all sensibility and sense of oneness of our spirit, soul and body in cooperation with the Lord. We repent for becoming and having the most hardened of hearts. We repent for deliberately stepping into something dark and for agreeing to have no conscience.

We repent for allowing ourselves to be void of truth. We repent for taking up the other crowns and then wearing this one last. We repent for the lust of blood, the drinking of blood, and the eating of flesh from the kingdom of darkness. We are only to take in the blood and body of Christ. We repent for ourselves and our generations. We repent for the idea of getting near the unholy fire and letting it burn us and for basking in it, allowing it to consume us.

We request that all crowns be destroyed and that this specific crown be fully removed and destroyed, as we have done the repentance work. We request the full removal of this vile crown from our heads as well as from the heads of our generations. We ask that it be burned in the Holy Fire of the Lord God Almighty.

We request the amendment of 'As if it Never Were' and ask for restoration in the mighty name of Jesus.

Please burn the spiritual residue, essences, and debris. In Jesus' name, we ask for the Superior Crowns of the Kingdom of Heaven to be placed on our heads, overturning the egregiousness of our sins.

We ask for Your righteous verdict, Your honor, or further counsel.

> [If further counsel is advised, follow these instructions. Once you have received a righteous verdict, begin the following segment:]

We speak to the Earth on which every one of our generations has stepped, including those related to us by blood, marriage, adoption, or civil and religious covenant.

Earth, we have received a righteous verdict from the Courts of Heaven this day. We bless you to hear the word of the Lord. We bless you to swallow up the iniquity and the egregious sins of self-deception and wearing these crowns. Swallow up every word and deed that was done upon you. Swallow the innocent bloodshed, sexual sins, moving of the boundary stones, worship of ourselves, idol worship, occultic worship, theft—every sin under the sun that Jesus died for. We charge you to swallow it up and bless you to your original design. We bless you to see the governing sons and to begin blessing us. Begin pouring out your riches of abundance of truth and life.

We request the blood of Jesus to cover every place this was done upon you or in you. We speak to the frequencies of the wind to blow away the evil, to the water to drown it, and to the fire to burn it. We speak to you to return to your original design as the Lord had created you. The Earth is the Lord's, and its fullness belongs to the Lord.

We speak peace. We thank the Just Judge. We thank you, Jesus, the author and the finisher of our faith, for the Crowns of Righteousness and the Crown of Love that trump this inferior crown.

As governing sons, we pick up these Superior Crowns, place them upon our heads, and ask You to help us rule. We commission the angels to render these righteous verdicts in the spirit and the natural. We commission the angels to put this on record.

Thank You, Just Judge, for honoring us and trusting us with the responsibility of wearing these Crowns of Love and Righteousness. Thank You for helping us occupy the territory You assigned us. We don't take this lightly and ask for supernatural assistance and help daily to govern well as Your sons, in the name of Jesus.

As a son, we call in the treasure that has been lost from the north, the south, the east, and the west in every age, realm, dimension, and time to fill the capacity of this section.

We ask that all of this be done in time and out of time, and in every age, realm, and dimension, and that all of the spiritual debris, residue, and essences that were left behind by this inferior crown and the spirits that came with it be destroyed utterly. We thank You, Father, for what You did, Jesus, for giving us authority and dominion here.

——— ∞ ———

Chapter 9
The Hierarchical Structure of the Seven False Crowns

Ruling Crowns:

- **Fear**: "Superior in its inferiority," ruling over many lesser crowns.
- **Devouring**: The ultimate crown that cannot be removed until others are addressed first.
- **Antichrist**: Coordinates the religious deception system.

Supporting Crowns:

- **Deception, Secrets, Magic, and Loathing**: Create conditions that amplify the ruling crowns' effectiveness.

The Escalation Game:
How One Crown Leads to Another

Here's something that should get your attention: these crowns have a **gateway effect**! We are explicitly warned that "those who wear this crown can easily put on the Crown of Deception." It's like spiritual drug addiction—you start with something that seems minor, but it opens the door to progressively worse bondage.

- Fear makes you vulnerable to accepting other false solutions.
- Deception prepares your mind to accept even bigger lies.
- Minor compromises create major spiritual disasters.

Some Crowns Rule Others

Not all crowns are created equal! There is a defined spiritual hierarchy.

The Ruling Crowns

- **Fear** is "superior in its inferiority" and rules over many other inferior crowns.
- **Devouring** is the ultimate crown that "cannot be removed until other crowns are removed first."
- **Antichrist** appears to coordinate the entire religious deception system.

Deception, Secrets, Magic, and Loathing create the conditions that make the ruling crowns more effective.

These crowns have actual **spiritual technology**!

- Magic has a built-in "eye" that monitors everything the wearer does (creepy, right?).
- Secrets operate sophisticated surveillance systems.
- Fear uses "technology" that disrupts spiritual frequencies.
- Multiple crowns interfere with your ability to hear God's voice.

It is as though Satan has constructed his own spiritual equivalent of an intelligence-gathering agency operating in the unseen realm!

The Targeting System: How They Hunt You

Each crown has specific hunting strategies:

Vulnerability Hunters:

- **Fear** targets trauma, generational wounds, and fractured identity.
- **Devouring** literally "sniffs out the weak" and follows the "stench of sin."
- **Magic** uses "allure" and false beauty to attract victims.

Identity Attacks:

- **Deception** attacks through "all the selves" (self-righteousness, self-hatred, etc.).
- **Antichrist** creates a false superiority identity.
- **Secrets** exploits the wound of orphanhood—"not knowing their Father."

The Ultimate Endgame

Here's what really got my attention about the ultimate goals:

Total Spiritual Destruction

- **Antichrist's** main mission is **"to bring an end to the embodiment of the church."**
- **Devouring** seeks **"whom he may devour" for complete annihilation.**
- **Loathing** literally **"eats you alive and consumes you."**

Complete Separation from God: They're not just trying to make you sin—they want to completely replace your relationship with God with a counterfeit system of self-worship and false spirituality.

Why This Matters:
The Strategic Advantage

Understanding these connections gives you a HUGE advantage! Instead of fighting seven separate battles, you can recognize the network and address it systematically. Since the crowns support each other, there's actually a strategic order for removing them. Devouring cannot be removed until the others are dismantled first. This process mirrors dismantling a bomb—you must cut the correct wires in the correct order. These aren't random individual problems—they're a coordinated system designed to trap you in systematic deception. Recognizing the connections helps you develop comprehensive freedom strategies.

The Network Effect. These aren't individual problems, but a coordinated network designed to trap people in systematic deception. Understanding their connections helps in developing comprehensive freedom strategies rather than addressing symptoms individually.

The Ultimate Battle. This seven-crown system is a counterfeit kingdom constructed to oppose and replace authentic Kingdom authority. Satan is not merely attempting to influence individuals; he is attempting to substitute God's government with a false, corrupt system.

The encouraging truth is that recognizing these patterns and connections empowers you to address them systematically through the Courts of Heaven, breaking the entire network rather than fighting individual battles!

Here's the beautiful part: you're not fighting this battle alone, and you're definitely not powerless!

The same Jesus who defeated Satan at the cross has given you authority to:

- Recognize these patterns and connections.
- Address them systematically through the Courts of Heaven.
- Break the entire network rather than fighting individual symptoms.
- Replace false crowns with authentic Kingdom authority.

This seven-crown system might be
Satan's counterfeit kingdom,
but ***greater is He who is in you***
than he who is in the world!

You've got the inside scoop on how the enemy's system works, the legal authority to dismantle it, and the Superior Crowns of the Kingdom to replace it with. This is not merely hope—it is a victory strategy.

Take heart. Understanding the enemy's playbook is the first step toward complete freedom. You are already moving toward wearing the authentic crowns that belong to you as a son or daughter of the King!

The Ultimate Battle

This seven-crown system represents a complete counterfeit kingdom designed to oppose and replace authentic Kingdom authority. The goal isn't just individual bondage but the systematic replacement of God's government with Satan's false system.

The encouraging truth is that recognizing these patterns and connections empowers you to address them systematically through the Courts of Heaven, breaking the entire network rather than fighting individual battles!

———— ∞ ————

Chapter 10
Prayer of Freedom from the Seven False Crowns

If you have prayed the prayers of freedom from all seven of the false crowns, you may want to wrap up the prayer work in this manner:

Father, we ask to step into Your Court of Crowns. We ask that the accuser of the brethren be brought into this court as well as our generations, those related to us by blood, marriage, civil and religious covenant, all the way back to Your hand in the Garden and all the way forward to as far as it needs to go.

We ask that the seven-headed dragon be brought in, muzzled and caged. We request that the accuser of the brethren and every Principality, power, demon, ruler of darkness, and evil entity that was associated with the seven-headed dragon, their inferior crowns, mantles, altars, thrones, and scepters, be brought in and gagged as well.

Having done repentance work for each of the seven crowns, Your Honor, we are asking that the repentance work already accomplished, and the verdicts be brought into evidence in this court this day. We also request our cloud of witnesses, the angels and every witness to these events be brought into this court on our behalf.

We request that these seven heads be judged today, for they have inflicted pain, torment, anguish, and untold misery upon Your sons and daughters and the peoples of the Earth. They have hindered the growth, abilities, expansion, and work of Your church on Earth. They have murdered, stolen, and destroyed without regard for You, Your sons, or Your purposes in the Earth. They have laid evil and egregious crowns on the heads of Your sons to mock not only them but You.

We ask that each head be judged, cut off, and destroyed from our lives, and the damage be undone via the amendment of 'As if it Never Were.'

We ask that You please burn the inferior Crown of the Beast, which is set above the seven-headed dragon, the dragon, its seven heads, its inferior crowns, thrones, mantles, scepters, altars, spiritual residue, essences, and debris. In Jesus' name, we ask for the Superior Crowns of the Kingdom of Heaven to be placed on our heads, overturning the egregiousness of our sins.

We ask for renewed authorization for every crown restored to us and those to be restored today in Your court.

We are grateful to Heaven for revealing the red dragon, its inferior crowns, associated evil entities, and its mission. We are grateful that Revelation tells us that this dragon has been pierced by God Himself. Thank you for your kindness in helping us overcome by the word of our testimony and the blood of the lamb.

We ask that all of this be done in time and out of time, and in every age, realm, and dimension, and that all the spiritual debris, residue, and essences that were left behind by this inferior crown and the spirits that came with it be destroyed utterly. We also ask that these evil entities be judged in Your court this day, in Jesus' name.

We thank You, Father, for what You did, Jesus, for giving us the authority and dominion here.

———— ∞ ————

Chapter 11

The Seven False Crowns Network: A Systematic Analysis

Nearly every crown operates from a foundation of pride—the same spiritual weakness that caused Satan's fall. This creates a reliable entry point into human hearts, with pride serving as the "root system" that feeds all other deceptive patterns.

Universal Strategy: Contaminated Counterfeits

All seven crowns employ the same core deception: they appear beneficial but are spiritually contaminated. Like appealing food laced with poison, these crowns present attractive facades while delivering spiritual toxins.

Primary Goal: Strategic Isolation

Every crown serves one devastating purpose: separation from truth, healthy relationships, and God.

This isolation creates vulnerability to additional deception through a divide-and-conquer strategy.

Strategic Alliances

The Religious Deception Trinity: Deception + Secrets + Antichrist form the **primary church infiltration system,** corrupting spiritual leadership and promoting false authority.

The Control Syndicate: Fear + Magic + Secrets creates comprehensive manipulation through vulnerability, false solutions, and hidden information.

The Supremacy Alliance: Deception + Antichrist + Loathing generate superiority complexes through grandiose delusions, elitist attitudes, and hatred of opposition.

Escalation Patterns

The crowns operate with a **gateway effect**—minor compromises open doors to major bondage. Fear creates vulnerability to other crowns, while Deception prepares minds for the Antichrist crown. When multiple crowns combine, they produce exponentially amplified damage.

Targeting and Surveillance Systems

Each crown employs specific hunting strategies and spiritual surveillance technology. They target trauma, generational wounds, identity vulnerabilities, and spiritual orphanhood while monitoring and disrupting the wearer's spiritual frequencies.

Ultimate Endgame

The complete system aims for total spiritual destruction and systematic replacement of God's government with Satan's counterfeit kingdom. The goal extends beyond individual bondage to the elimination of authentic church embodiment.

Strategic Advantage Through Recognition

Understanding these interconnected patterns enables systematic dismantling rather than fighting individual symptoms. Like defusing a bomb, there's a specific order for removal, recognizing that this coordinated network can be addressed comprehensively through spiritual authority rather than fragmented battles.

The False Crown Network: How Satan's Seven-Crown System Really Works

After diving deep into all seven false crowns, I've discovered some fascinating (and eye-opening!) patterns about how these spiritual counterfeits work together. Think of it like uncovering a massive conspiracy—except this one's been operating in the spiritual realm for centuries!

The Foundation: It All Starts with Pride

Nearly every single crown has pride as its foundation! It's like pride is the spiritual "root system" that feeds all the others. The Crown of Deception is literally "based on pride," while Antichrist creates those "I'm better than you" attitudes, Magic feeds that insatiable "lust for power," and Secrets operates through grandiosity.

It is diabolically strategic: attack the very thing that caused Satan's own fall and you gain a reliable entry point into human hearts.

The Deception Network: A Master Deception Strategy

What is brilliant—though evil—about this system is that every crown operates through the same core strategy: **they all appear good but are completely contaminated**. It is spiritual food poisoning; the meal looks delicious and smells amazing, but it is loaded with toxins!

- **Deception** + **Secrets** + **Antichrist** form a powerful trinity of religious deception.
- **Fear** creates "distorted thinking" while seeming protective.

- **Magic** "seems good but is contaminated by darkness."
- **Antichrist** "clings to the cross but in defilement."
- **Secrets** create "delusions of grandeur" that feel empowering.
- **Antichrist** specifically "works with the **Crown of Secrets and Crown of Deceit.**"
- This network **infiltrates churches** through "Freemasonry and Eastern Star."
- All three promote **false spiritual authority and religious pride.**

No wonder people get trapped! These crowns are master illusionists.

The Isolation Game

Every single crown has one devastating goal: **separation**. They're all designed to isolate you from truth, healthy relationships, and most importantly, from God. It's like they're running the ultimate divide-and-conquer strategy:

- **Fear** blocks your ability to receive from Heaven.
- **Loathing** makes civil conversation impossible.
- **Secrets** silences the very voice of God through you.
- **Magic** suspends you in false spiritual realms.
- **Antichrist** actually drives people permanently away from the church.

Isolation makes you vulnerable to even more deception. Brilliant? Yes. Evil? Absolutely.

The Strategic Partnerships: Crown Alliances

These crowns do not operate alone. They form specific alliances—spiritual crime syndicates:

- **Deception** creates "delusions of grandeur."
- **Antichrist** produces "better than you" attitudes.
- **Loathing** generates "intense hatred" of opposition.

This alliance is particularly dangerous in leadership positions, where it can weaponize authority against the people of God.

The "Religious Deception Mafia"

Deception + **Secrets** + **Antichrist** = The ultimate church infiltration team!

Crown of Antichrist "works with the Crown of Secrets and Crown of Deceit." This trio specializes in corrupting spiritual leadership through Freemasonry and Eastern Star connections. They are a core reason behind so many church scandals and fallen leaders.

The “Control and Manipulation Syndicate”

Fear + Magic + Secrets = The perfect control system! Fear makes you vulnerable, Magic offers false power as the “solution,” and Secrets maintains control through hidden information. All three are described as “master manipulators” who create unbreakable strongholds.

The “Supremacy Alliance”

Deception + Antichrist + Loathing = The superiority complex dream team! Deception creates “delusions of grandeur,” Antichrist produces “better than you” attitudes, and Loathing generates “intense hatred” toward anyone who disagrees. This is particularly deadly in positions of authority.

Sequential Progression (Gateway Effect)

- Minor crowns open doors to major ones.
- Text explicitly states: “The ones who wear this crown can easily put on the Crown of Deception.”
- Fear makes people vulnerable to other crowns.
- Deception prepares people for the Antichrist crown.

Once this sequence begins, bondage escalates rapidly.

Amplification Effects

- Devouring works "in tandem with all other crowns"—it is the ultimate amplifier.
- When multiple crowns combine, they create exponentially more damage.
- The seven-headed dragon represents the complete system working together as one counterfeit kingdom.

This is not random. It is structured and intentionally synergistic.

——— ∞ ———

Chapter 12
Epilogue

As we have learned throughout this book, Heaven possesses strategies capable of overcoming every tactic and operation of hell. As the sons gain wisdom from Heaven and learn to effectively engage and defeat the forces of darkness, much that has been delayed by our enemies will be overcome.

Much of the spiritual warfare of the past was fruitless and failed to produce the desired results. One key reason is that it was often attempted in our own strength rather than in partnership with the strength of the Hosts of Heaven—the angel armies trained and equipped for these battles. Whenever men attempted to perform tasks assigned to angels, the angelic armies simply waited for proper instruction. The problem was that we did not know how to instruct them. We did not understand, recognize, or utilize their great might and wisdom in warfare.

We also did not understand the false crowns and their structure and hierarchy. It is my hope that this information will help you understand better what you are dealing with as you go forth as a son and conquer.

A principle of Scripture is that *what we honor, we receive the benefit of.* The truth is, we did not honor the angelic realm, and therefore we did not receive the benefit of what they could do. We may have invited them to the battle, but we did not release them to do what they do best—defeat enemies. We owe them an apology.

We knew nothing of co-laboring with our angels or with the angels assigned to regions. We knew little or nothing about how to direct them in battle via praying in tongues. Consequently, many battles were waged and lost because of these misunderstandings.

The good news is that now we have learned. We have gained understanding of the Courts of Heaven and how to address legal issues tied to specific regions. We have learned how to resolve matters in the Courts. We have learned about the inferior crowns the workers of darkness wear and the superiority of the crowns given to the sons and their angels. We have discovered how inferior crowns form alliances to defeat the saints, and how the saints can dismantle these alliances and secure victory.

Victory is imminent for the sons as we access the strategies of Heaven and release the Hosts of Heaven to do battle for the Kingdom. Let's proceed to victory!

——— ∞ ———

Appendix

Learning to Live Spirit First

A challenge with how we were taught about the Christian life is that everything was put off until sometime in the future. Then, we read the letters of Paul, and we experienced a disconnect. Heaven, to us, was a destination, not a resource. We knew nothing about learning to live from our spirits. We only knew what we had been doing all our lives since birth, and that was to live to satisfy our soul or our flesh. We sorely need to learn an alternative way of living.

Exchanging Our Way of Living

Paul recorded these words in his letter to the Romans:

> *Those who are motivated by the flesh only pursue what benefits themselves. But those who live by the impulses of the Holy Spirit are motivated to pursue spiritual realities. (Romans 8:5, TPT)*

We must learn to live spirit first! We must exchange our way of living. We must learn to live from our spirit. We need to understand the hierarchy within us:

a. We are a spirit.
b. We possess a soul.
c. We live in a body.

Each component has a specific purpose in our lives. Our spirit is the interface with the supernatural realm. It is designed for interfacing with Heaven and the Kingdom realm. Our spirit has been in existence in our body since conception. Our soul has a different purpose. It communicates to our intellect and our physical body what our spirit has obtained from Heaven. It is the interface with our body. Our body houses the two components and follows the dictates of whichever component is dominating,

Most of us have never been taught about having our spirit dominate. Rather, we have merely assumed that our soul being dominant was the required mode of operation.

Our soul always wants to be in charge. Our soul is susceptible to carnal or fleshly desires, lusts, and behaviors. It will, at times, resist our spirit and body. It must be made to submit to our spirit by an act of our will.

Our will is a means of instructing either component (spirit, soul, or body) in what to do. Our soul has a will, and so does our spirit. We choose who dominates!

Our body, on the other hand, has appetites that will control us in subjection to our soul. They become partners in crime—remember that second piece of chocolate cake it wanted? Our body will try, along with our soul, to dictate our behavior. It will likely resist the spirit's domination of our lives. However, it will obey our spirit's domination if instructed, and our body can aid our spirit if trained to do so.

The typical expression that operates in most people's lives is that their soul is first, body second, and their spirit is somewhere in the distance in last place.

In some people, especially those very conscious of their physical fitness or physical appearance, there is a different lineup. Their body is their priority, the soul second, and again, their spirit is the lowest priority.

Heaven's desire for us is vastly different. Heaven desires that we live spirit first, soul second, and body third. Since we are spiritual beings, this is the optimal arrangement. For most of us, our spirit was not activated in our lives in any measure until we became born again.

If, after our salvation experience, we began to pursue our relationship with the Father, then we became much more aware of our spirit and learned to live more spirit-conscious. The apostle Paul wrote in his various epistles about living in the spirit or walking in the spirit.

Because we are spiritual beings, our spirits cry out for a deepening of relationship with the Father.

Our spirit longs for it and will try to steer us in that direction. Many of us had a hunger for God from an early age.

Our soul has certain characteristics that explain its behavior in our lives. This is the briefest of lists, but I think we will get the idea. Our soul is selfish. It wants what it wants when it wants it. It can be very pouty. It can act like a small child. It is offendable and often even looks for opportunities to be offended. Our soul is also rude.

Our bodies have different sets of characteristics. It is inconsiderate, demanding, lazy, and self-serving. It does not want to get out of bed in the morning for many people. In others, it wants to be fed things that are not beneficial.

However, the characteristics of our spirit are hugely different. If we live out of our spirit, we will find that we are loving and prone to be gentle. We desire peace. We are considerate. We are far more contented when living out of our spirit. Also, joy will often have a great expression in our lives.

Sometimes, we have experienced traumas that create a situation of our soul not trusting our spirit. The soul blames the spirit for not protecting it. The irony is that, typically, our soul never gave place to the spirit so that it could protect us. The soul places false blame on the spirit, and it must be coerced to forgive the spirit. Then, the soul must relinquish control to the spirit. Once the soul forgives the spirit, the two components can begin to work in harmony.

If I were to flash an image of some delicious, freshly cooked donuts in front of us, what would happen? For many, their body would announce a craving for one. What if, instead, I showed an image of a bowl of broccoli? How many people would get excited about that? Probably not as much excitement over a bowl of broccoli would be exhibited. Which does our body prefer—the donuts or the broccoli? For the untamed soul, the donuts are likely to win out every time. Which do most kids prefer?

In any case, we can train ourselves to go for the healthier option. A principle regarding this that I heard years ago is summed up like this:

What we feed will live—
what we starve will die

What do we want to be dominant—our spirit, our soul, or our body? The part we feed will dominate.

For some, they feed their soul and live by the logic of their mind. Everything must be reasoned out in their mind before they will accept it. However, because our soul gains its insight from the Tree of the Knowledge of Good and Evil, it will always have faulty and limited understandings.

How do we change this soul-dominant or body-dominant pattern? We instruct our soul to back up, and we call our spirit to come forward. Some people may need to physically stand up and speak to our soul and say, "Soul, back up," and as they say those words, take a physical step backward. Then, speak to their spirit out loud and say, "Spirit, come forward." As we speak those words, take a physical step forward. This prophetic act helps trigger a shift within them.

Live spirit first!

Benefits of Living Spirit First

Why would we want to live spirit first? Let me present several reasons. Living spirit first will create in us an increased awareness of Heaven and the realms of Heaven. It will create a deeper comprehension of the presence of Holy Spirit, of angels, and men and women in white linen. We will be able to better hear the voice of Heaven. We will experience greater creativity, productivity, hope, and peace. We will become more aware of the needs of people that we meet.

As we live spirit first, we will be able to access the riches of Heaven in our life. Petty things that formerly bothered us will dissipate in importance or impact in our lives. We will be able to move ahead, not concerned with the petty, mundane, or unproductive things that have affected our lives before we begin to live spirit first.

This way of life is more than a game changer—for the believer, it is the only way to live. We will face challenges as we build our business or live our life from Heaven down, but we will more readily be able to access the solutions of Heaven as we live with an awareness of the richness of Heaven and all that is available to us as a son or daughter of the Lord Most High. Do not live dominated by the soul. *Live **spirit** first!*

———— ∞ ————

Resources from LifeSpring International Ministries

A visit to the **RonHorner.com** website will give a glimpse of the various branches of ministry we are involved in. We started providing coaching to people within the Courts of Heaven, advocating for them and their situations. Our corporate name is LifeSpring International Ministries, Inc., a North Carolina registered nonprofit corporation.

Personal Advocacy Sessions

Known as Personal Advocacy Sessions, these 90-minute sessions with our trained team of advocates have successfully worked with a myriad of situations. If you have an issue that you can't seem to get breakthrough about, schedule a session with our advocates.

LifeSpring Mentoring Group

Since starting this weekly class on Zoom in 2019, we have taught on the Courts of Heaven, protocols, engaging Heaven for revelation, working with angels and men and women white linen, lingering human spirits, and more. It is a free class. Simply visit **ronhorner.com** to register for the link for the class.

Membership Program

We have several tiers of membership for those tracking with us. The Platinum level gains you access to our library of videos, blogs, and more.

LifeSpring School of Ministry

A trimester-based school to help you grow in your walk. Trimester 1 focuses on cleansing your generations. Trimester 2 focuses on Protocols of the Courts of Heaven, and Trimester 3 focuses on Advanced Protocols of the Courts of Heaven. Completion of Trimesters 1, 2, and 3 will qualify the student for consideration as a Junior or Senior Advocate able to conduct Personal Advocacy Sessions with our clients.

AfterCare

Not every situation is solved by the Courts of Heaven. Sometimes, people need to learn simple things to navigate life. Our AfterCare program provides Biblical counseling (not Courts of Heaven focused), classes, and groups regularly.

Crown Ecclesia

In 2022, we started a Sunday Gathering now known as Crown Ecclesia We meet weekly at 11:00 AM Eastern, and on the first Sunday of the month, we have an afternoon gathering to do legislative work in the Courts of Heaven as a group. All are welcome. Simply visit **crownecclesia.com** and register for the link.

Heaven Down Business

Heaven Down Business is a worldwide coaching and consultancy business designed to assist entrepreneurs and business owners in implementing the Heaven Down™ Business Building paradigm into their business. For more information, visit: **heavendownbusiness.com**.

Adina's Melodies/Heaven Down Music

Adina Horner, co-founder of LifeSpring, is a gifted minstrel and has several albums of prophetic worship music available on several of the most popular music platforms. Visit **adinasmelodies.com**.

LifeSpring Publishing/Scroll Publishers

LifeSpring Publishing focuses on Dr. Ron's titles, while Scroll Publishing serves as our imprint for authors whose work explores engaging Heaven, living spirit forward, and the Heaven Down™ lifestyle.

YouTube Channel

Our most recent videos from the Mentoring Group are posted on YouTube®. Visit our YouTube® channel, **courtsofheavenwebinar** on YouTube® for the latest videos.

RonHorner.com

Our website, **RonHorner.com,** has a myriad of resources and videos, many of which are free.

——— ∞ ———

Description

The spiritual battles you face aren't random—they're part of a strategic alliance designed to keep you from your calling. This groundbreaking book exposes seven false crowns that work together to undermine believers: Deception, Fear, Loathing, Devouring, Magic, Secrets, and Antichrist.

Through powerful heavenly encounters and biblical teaching, you'll discover how to identify these crowns operating in your life, understand their specific tactics and structures, and break free through Courts of Heaven protocols. Learn why Fear serves as the "master controller," how Magic uses beauty to deceive, and why Antichrist has infiltrated even churches.

More than identifying problems, this book equips you with practical solutions: breaking generational curses, partnering with angels, mitigating territorial strongholds, and operating as Heaven's problem-solver on earth. God has commissioned you to remove obstacles blocking His Kingdom advancement.

The false crowns may be sophisticated, but they're no match for believers who understand their strategies and enforce Christ's victory.

It's time to reject the enemy's counterfeit and embrace the authentic Crown of Authority Jesus freely gives His sons and daughters.

———— ∞ ————

About the Author

Dr. Ron Horner is an apostolic teacher specializing in the Courts of Heaven and divine revelation. He has written nearly forty books on the Courts of Heaven, engaging Heaven, working with angels, or living from revelation.

He currently trains people to engage with the Courts of Heaven in a weekly online teaching session. You can register to participate and discover more about the Courts of Heaven prayer paradigm on his various websites, classes, products, and services found here:

www.ronhorner.com

———— ∞ ————

Other Books by Dr. Ron M. Horner

Building Your Business from Heaven Down

Building Your Business from Heaven Down 2.0

Building Your Business with the Blueprint of Heaven

Commissioning Angels – Volume 1

Cooperating with The Glory

Dealing with Trusts & Consequential Liens in the Courts of Heaven

Embracing Crowns for Governmental Intercession

Embracing Crowns for Your Business

Embracing Crowns for Your Family

Embracing Your Crown of Authority

Engaging Angels in the Realms of Heaven

Engaging Heaven for Revelation – Volume 1

Engaging Heaven for Revelation – Volume 2

Engaging Heaven for Trade

Engaging the Courts for Ownership & Order

Engaging the Courts for Your City (*Paperback, Leader's Guide & Workbook*)

Engaging the Courts of Healing & the Healing Garden

Engaging the Courts of Heaven

Engaging the Help Desk of the Courts of Heaven

Four Keys to Defeating Accusations (Second Edition)

Freedom from Mithraism

Kingdom Dynamics – Volume 1

Kingdom Dynamics – Volume 2

Let's Get it Right!

Lingering Human Spirits

Lingering Human Spirits – Volume 2

Living Spirit Forward (Second Edition)

Maximizing Your Crown of Authority

Next Dimension Access to the Court of Supplications

Overcoming the False Verdicts of Freemasonry (Fourth Edition)

Overcoming Verdicts from the Courts of Hell

Principles of Kingdom Advancement

Releasing Bonds from the Courts of Heaven (Second Edition)

Strategic Alliances of the Seven False Crowns

The Courts of Heaven: An Introduction (Third Edition) *formerly known as* Engaging the Mercy Court of Heaven

The Courts of Heaven Process Charts

Unlocking Spiritual Seeing

Working with Your Realms and Your Realm Angels

SPANISH

Cómo Anular los Falsos Veredictos de la Masonería

Cómo Proceder en la Corte Celestial de Misericordia

Cómo Proceder en las Cortes para su Ciudad

Cómo Trabajar con Angeles en los Ambitos del Cielo

Cooperando con La Gloria de Dios

Las Cuatro Llaves para Anular las Acusaciones

Liberando Bonos en las Cortes Celestiales

Liberando Su Visión Espiritual

Sea Libre del Mitraísmo

Tablas de Proceso de la Cortes del Cielo

——— ∞ ———

www.ingramcontent.com/pod-product-compliance
Lightning Source LLC
LaVergne TN
LVHW090937080826
845145LV00003B/781